UP CUTSHIN AND DOWN GREASY

UP CUTSHIN

and

DOWN GREASY

LEONARD W. ROBERTS

Folkways of a Kentucky
Mountain Family

University of Kentucky Press

PUBLICATION of this book has been aided by a grant from The Ford Foundation. Printed at the University of Kentucky. Library of Congress catalog card number 59-10277.

TO MY MOTHER

RHODA JANE OSBORN ROBERTS

PREFACE

The Pine Mountain range slices across the extreme southeastern border of Kentucky, isolating Bell and Harlan counties from the rest of the state. That is, it once isolated these counties—before the good timber and coal were needed to move the nation's industries. Now a fine road, U.S. Highway 119, and the Louisville and Nashville Railroad wind up the Cumberland River from the knobs of the lowlands to the head of the river. Along these lines of communication are county seats of 5,000 population and mining towns and lumber camps of a few hundred houses each.

But across the long ridge of Pine Mountain to the northwest lie the most isolated acres of the state—on the headwaters of the Kentucky River. Here are such picturesque branches and valleys as Cutshin, Greasy, and Big Leatherwood. Here I have explored for a decade, discovering many strange and lingering folkways, primitive farming and folk handicrafts, lumbering and hunting, funeralizing and moonshining. The most valuable treasure that I have found, however, has been an old-fashioned family tradition of Old World folktale telling and ancient ballad singing. On a small branch of Cutshin Creek I met Mandy Couch Hendrix, who directed me back across the Pine ridge to Putney on the Cumberland, a stringtown lumber camp some eight miles above Harlan, to her brothers Jim and Dave Couch, who recorded for me the family store of folklore—sixty old tales and one hundred folksongs and hymns.

I managed recording sessions with the two brothers about every month during most of 1952. After a lapse of one year I returned to the search with Jim, who guided me about the region to other members of the family tree, including two trips to his cousin Joe's in Appalachia, Virginia. Finally, I tried to

terminate the collecting phase of my work with the two
brothers in the fall of 1955, with their lore still unexhausted.

The next phase, the transcribing of family narrative, story,
and song, began in the winter of 1955. The mass of material
proved to be too large for a single study, and so I have divided
it into two parts: family narrative, and family stories and songs.
Though recorded at many different times, the family narrative
has been integrated, and I have remained in the background,
allowing the Couches to tell their various family experiences in
their own words. The discrepancies in such data as number of
children and historical dates I have not attempted to reconcile,
except for an occasional explanation in brackets.

The main body of material in this volume, therefore, is the
simple history and folkways of this mountain family, their
daily life in work and play, in joy and sorrow. To illustrate
their telling and singing techniques I have included some
typical stories and songs in the last chapter. The entire collection of tales and songs, including music and fairly exhaustive
notes to all items, has been issued as no. 30 in the Kentucky
Microcards, series A, also published by the University of Kentucky Press. There the folklorist will find the material faith-
fully transcribed, with bibliography, parallels, and motif and
type numbers for his research purposes.

I hope the reader finds as much pleasure and profit in reading
the following pages as I experienced in my four years of
hospitality among the Couch folk.

L. W. R.

CONTENTS

CHAPTER 1

JIM COUCH, HIS FAMILY STORY

PUTNEY, a stringtown along the winding Cumberland River, grew around the old seat of one of the largest sawmills in eastern Kentucky. I can remember well the day I came over from Pine Mountain School to find Jim Couch, a storyteller from back on the headwaters of the Kentucky River, who was said to know all the stories of the clan of tellers and ballad singers. The houses became thicker along the blacktop, and soon I could see the chimneys of the Intermountain Lumber and Coal Company pouring out acrid smoke on the wind. The level bottoms along the Poor Fork of the Cumberland were covered with acres of lumber stacks. After some inquiry I found where Jim lived and stopped by the road. His home was propped on the hillside in a small drain. I saw three working men on the lower porch and heard the cry of playing children in the lower yard behind a paling fence. I hallooed from the slat gate. A friendly response came from one of the men sitting in a low chair. He was black as a minstrel from his hard-toed shoes to his mining cap.

I entered the yard and clambered up the steps to the end of the porch. Two of the men (I later learned they were Jim's brothers Alex and Harrison) rose, and after speaking to me, they went to their homes below the road. The seated man waved a black hand to a split-bottom chair, where I sat facing him. "Been over to Cutshin Creek," I began, "saw your sister Mandy. She tells me you know a lot of stories—know all the stories of the family."

"Yeaw," he said, "I used to tell all the old stories that our mother handed down while she was a-raising us. But I've not told them, some of 'em in years. About forgot 'em."

As I enlarged upon my interest in the old handed-down folkstories, Jim removed his hard mining helmet and his heavy electric battery, belt and all, and hung them aside. And then he began to undress in earnest. Off came the hard shoe and sock from one leg, and then the caked overall pants. He unfastened a smooth leather belt from his middle and unlaced a leather casing from his upper leg. Finally he took off a whole leg, shoe and all, and set it against the wall. My line of talk died away. He took up the conversation by explaining, "Lost my leg a few years ago in the mines. Got it caught between two cars. The doc had to take it off. I've been following mining for nine year now."

"What did you do before entering the mines?"

He hung his wet, faded chambray shirt on the back of a chair. "Why, I used to be a lumberman. Worked for this lumber company for nineteen year—from here to lower Greasy Creek. I learnt to measure lumber at the stacks—I was a lumber scaler for my last ten years with 'em." Before I could lead him on much further he said, "Wait till I get my bath. I have to get this black offen me before I can do a thing when I come in."

I waited while he hopped from chair to doorfacing and into the living room, where he squatted in an old oblong tub on the floor. While I looked across the way to the peaks of Big Black Mountain, I could hear his wife pouring water and tempering it to Jim's notion. On first impression Jim was a slight man, as mountain men go, but he was actually of average build. What I had seen of his face was ruddy, and his eyes had a keen and mischievous look about them. His voice was low and rich, with a good flexible vocabulary and mountain idiom. I knew he was fifty, but his crop of still black hair did not show his age, except for the slight receding and parting line across the top. The face was slightly long, as was his head, and I had been aware of prominent high cheekbones. When he hopped back out in clean colored clothes, he did not offer to replace his leg, but, sitting down, he threw the stump across an empty chair and grunted refreshingly.

In the next twenty or thirty minutes Jim ran over about four of the Old World folktales, enough to convince me that he and his family had kept in tradition a heritage of old tales. At this time and for many more sessions I asked him about his family and about his experiences in a mountain home. The following pages set forth what he related to me in his own words.

"Why, yeaw," he began, "I can trace our people back a good piece. My mother allas claimed that her people was Irish, and my daddy said the name of Couch was French. I don't know for sure when they come to this country, but that's what they allas claimed. I guess I know more about our generations than anybody else in the family. I've kept up with 'em and asked 'em questions all my life.

"My great-grandfather on my mother's side went by the name of old Pressley Harris, and he is said to have come from Ireland and settled in North Caroliny. That was back in the 1830's or 40's. And he settled in the mountains of North Caroliny. I don't know who he married, but my mother said her grandmother on the Turner side was a fullblooded Cherokee Indian. He never come to this part of the country till he was old and his chillern was growed and married and his wife dead. But some of his chillern come in here. My grandfather was Lewis, and he settled over here on Greasy Creek in Harlan County. He owned most of the land on what is known as Sang Branch. [*Sang* is from *ginseng,* a valuable medicinal root.] One of his girls, my mother, was named Mary Ann Harris. My father found her there and married her, and they inherited most of the Sang Branch.

"I was a purty good size chap when my great-grandfather died. He didn't know much of our language and never could read and write. He talked with a funny turn of speech, and he was a funny and a rowdy kind of a feller. Knowed more pranks and tricks than anybody nearly. Yeaw, he stayed around with us some and I've talked to him a lot.

"Now the Couches was French, my daddy allas said. My great-grandfather was Anse Couch, and he lived in Virginia, in the county of Scott. My grandfather was named John, and he married a Dutchman by the name of Sally Shepherd. Her mother was said to be a Wells. Grandfather John came in here and settled on Big Leatherwood 'way before the Civil War. When them troubles broke out, he went back to Virginia and fought through the Civil War on the Union side. Grandfather John came back and raised a big fambly, and one of his boys was named Tom—he is my father. He is living yet, up here in a cabin above my house. Getting up in years—he is ninety-two now. Married my mother on the Sang Branch, and they lived there for about ten years on that branch that had been deeded to my mother as her part of their inheritance. All you had to do back then was survey you out a piece of land and write up what was called a bond, take that and file it at the county seat, and get a patent and send it off to be recorded in Frankfort.

"Well, they was a land company here in Harlan town claimed all the land they could get a claim on and tried to go over patents and get a clearer title to it. That's what they done with my mother's holdings there on Sang Branch. They lawed for that piece of land. My father got holt of old Jedge Hall, and they beat them fellers and held the land. And then he turned right around and sold it out to one of them fellers. He went back to Leatherwood where he come from and raised us awhile on Clover Fork. We stayed there for several year, and then we moved here to Harlan County, to Nolansburg, where they was a big bandmill. By 1918 dad was a big logging contractor, and I worked on his crew. I went into the World War then and left my father to shift for hisself. My mother died in 1921. And now since we have been living here at Putney, dad has come here to live. He married again fifteen year ago when he was seventy-seven, and he has two chillern by his last wife; the youngest one, a boy, was born when he was eighty.

"Now sir, I'll tell you about my mother. She was just as good to people and treated 'em just as clever [hospitable] as anybody on the creek. Course she was proud of her fambly, and just like any woman in the hills she wouldn't have nothing to do with no men strangers. Always sunt 'em to dad. One time a man come to the house when she was there with just the least uns, and he wanted to set around till dad come in. And she told him she didn't want him to. He said something to her made her mad, and she run him off. Got the gun and told him she'd shoot him if he didn't take off for there.

"We was all kindy skittish about strangers that way. We got the idea they wanted to know our fambly affairs, or make fun of us. One time when the Pine Mountain Settlement School was just starting up, the school built a community house down there at the mouth of Big Laurel, and they would have us folks come in there and learn how to can stuff and how to take care of babies and such like. And some of them extension workers would come from Berea and lecture there. A bunch of women stayed there about two weeks oncet. And they got to asking the people to sing songs for 'em and tell stories. I was up there oncet, and they wanted me to tell some of my stories. I told 'em one, I told 'em Jack and the Bull Strap [microcard ed., No. 6],* and they took on about it and wanted more. I thought they was making fun, making us out as heathern or something, and I never went back up there and never told 'em another story.

"I guess I learnt to act that a-way from my mother. She was the storyteller in the fambly and would tell one about any time of a day or night. She would tell a story at the ends of corn rows while we was cooling and getting water, and of an

---

* Such references as this are to *The Tales and Songs of the Couch Family* (Kentucky Microcards, series A, no. 30, University of Kentucky Press, 1959). A list of the tales and songs is included in the Appendix of this book. For this particular story, see also Chapter 6.

evening around a gnat smoke in the yard and of a night before
bedtime. But the strange thing I noticed about her—she
wouldn't hardly tell stories when they was people at the house.
She'd just say, 'No, I'm not going to tell no stories.' And we
got so we wouldn't ask her before other people.

"We just lived as famblies, made all we got, and what we
couldn't get, we done without. We would go out the darkest,
rainiest night ever was and help a man in need, and we'd give
our last bite of grub—flour, sugar, medicine—to somebody need-
ing it. But let a man come around where he had no business
and never state his business, let him say something about us
or any of our people, and his hide would pay for it shore
as cat tracks.

"The people in the hills was not mean and didn't come
around to do anybody any dirt. They was all goodhearted
people that I ever knowed. And they didn't want to hide a
thing. We knowed the revenues and learnt how to spot 'em as
far as we could see 'em. We just didn't see strangers very often
—people we didn't know nary thing about—and we was allas
curious about 'em, and when one went through, we would ask
up and down who he was and what he was going through here
for. Maybe some house or store would be robbed, somebody
murdered on the road. Robbers, outlaws, foreigners come in
and get a place for the night and be gone. We'd talk about
them fellers for years.

"Now you want to hear about my brothers and sisters, and
I may as well start at the top and come down. The oldest one,
Lewis, he never got out of Harlan and Perry County in his life,
I don't guess. Lives over there on Laurel Fork o' Greasy and
has farmed all his life. He's got about eight chillern, or nine, I
don't just remember how many, a great gang of 'em he's raised.
My next brother, he took these here kindly epilepsy fits and
died when he was twenty-four year old, in the hospital at
Lexington, and was buried in Lexington graveyard. The next
one, Henry L., he got killed. He was a fine boy of fifteen when
we lived over there in Perry County, and he was out with a

man who dropped a pistol, and it went off and killed him. The next one was a girl—that is Mandy, who lived with us in Harlan till she married a Hendrix, and they settled over there where you saw her in Leslie County and has been there all her life. They raised I think it was eight chillern and has taken in one or two to raise. I stayed with her for years.

"The next one was a girl, too, but she died when she was four year old. And the next was Dave. He growed up about as I did, till he got married and settled in Leslie County, up till about ten year ago. He moved here to Harlan County and has been here ever since. They had twelve chillern and have done purty well, mining mostly since he come here, till a few years ago his eyes got to bothering him. He is purt nearly blind now and can't do no heavy work no more. Well, the next one is I. I married Stella Turner over there on Greasy Creek and we have six chillern. And the next one is Alex, who has lived here in Harlan County ever since he got up any size. Married and has got four chillern. Then comes another sister, Sally, and she married a Stewart and has lived around here most of her married life. She lives in a cabin 'way up over yander on the slope of Black Mountain, and they have now got fifteen chillern altogether. My baby brother lives right down here below the road, Harrison, and he's got four chillern—no, they've got five now. That makes three girls and seven boys old Tom the banjer picker had by my mother and two by his present wife. And altogether, when you count them all up, he has got fifty-nine grandchillern. Will probably have seventy-five.

"Ah, Lord, I'm such a mixture of French and Dutch, English and Irish and Indian, I've never been able to figure out just what I done and why I done it. I's so mean when I's growing up, I—I, it'd be a shame for a man to tell it, I guess. We was raised on a hillside farm, and it was just get up and work all day, and get out and play all night, about it. We raised everything we had, and if we hadn't a-raised it, we wouldn't a-got it. We allas had a big crap of corn for ourselves and our hogs and stock, and we raised beans and 'taters, cabbage, beets—everything that'd grow. Made our molasses into long sweetening and tapped the sugartrees for short sweetening. Ma made our soap out of hogs' guts and potash, and we raised broomcorn for our brooms. We allas had a big gang o' geese for our pillers and feather ticks, and we had guineas and ducks and chickens.

"What clothes we got, about all of 'em, was offen the sheep's wool. We allas had a big flock o' sheep and we'd drive 'em in of a spring and shear 'em. We little fellers would take the wool to the creek water and tromp it till it was clean, dry it, and help the girls pick the cuckleburs outten it. My mother, she'd card and spin her wool and weave it on a loom into purty good cloth. Then she'd set down and make us clothes. We'd take some wool off to the store and swap it to some eatables. But later, for several years, mother shipped some of her wool off and had it spun into skeins on the shears [shares], about half to come back to us and they kept the rest. The nearest railroad up till 1911 was at Pineville, about forty, fifty mile away. And they was another railhead at Hagan, Virginia, and to get there we went acrost Stone Mountain, Big and Little Black and Brush Mountains and up Catron's Creek, fifty, sixty mile, I guess.

"If my dad went to the railroad in the late summer, he would bring us back our only pair of shoes for the year. They was old brogans, went by the name of Tennessee Ties. Wear 'em from the first frost till barefoot time in the spring. Never needed half-soling; about the only thing to keep handy was some mutton or beef taller to keep 'em greased—till you could get 'em on—and off. Well, sometimes they would need a new pair of strings, and we would go out and ketch a groundhog, bring him in and tan his hide, make strings and harness leather outten it.

"In crap time dad would ketch the old mule and take a highfoot bull-tongue plow and start plowing in the balks of the corn. We'd hit that field about daylight and work till twelve. We didn't have no watches in them days—had an old striking clock but we couldn't pack it around. They was a poplar tree left in the field, and we had a marker on that tree. When the shadder of the sun got up to that marker, we would know that it was noontime. Come out to the house and eat dinner, rest awhile, and hit the field again. My mother would work with us evenings till about four o'clock and come out to do up the work and get supper. We would come out to the house, our clothes salty with sweat, and by suppertime the sun would be down behind the hills and cool air would be stirring in the valley. After supper at about dusky dark we would build up a gnat smoke out in the yard and set around in that smoke till ten o'clock and tell stories, sing songs. My mother would see that the milking was done and the dishes washed. She would come out in the yard in a chear, and we would start bagging her to tell us about old Jack in the Bean Tree [microcard ed., No. 1] or about the Little Black Hunchety Hunch [microcard ed., No. 4]. My dad would have one of us to bring out his old banjer—had a good un all his life. My grandfather made one that lasted for years. The box of it was made outten an old gourd. The strings was connected up some way on the neck, and that thing played right good, I thought. Pa would play Old Groundhog, Cold Frosty Morning, Shoo Fly, Arkansaw Traveler [microcard ed., Nos. 86, 89, 80, 87].

"Now we everyone, that is all seven of us at home, learnt to play that old banjer, even all the girls. It wouldn't take me long to learn a piece. I'd just watch him—watch my daddy note the strings and his fingers strike the chords, and then I'd grab the old banjer. I first learnt to play tunes by picking the strings while he noted 'em for me. My arms wouldn't be long enough to reach the neck. And I had an old plug banjer in my house all the time, up till just a few months ago. Swapped it off. Not long ago my daddy was down to the house, and I handed it to him. He was so old and nervous I didn't know what he could do with it. He took it in his arms and tried to play, but he couldn't even hit the strings. Brother Dave down here has one of our old banjers and he can play very well on it.

"Well, there's not nothing much to tell about me in the World War. I never did tell about it much. I went in when I was seventeen, volunteered, back in 1918, and was shipped to France right away. I fought through some of the hardest battles that won the war. I was wounded four times. And instead of coming back when it was over, I reenlisted. Stayed around over in France for some time and then got put into a casual detachment—digging up the dead soldiers and shipping them back to their states. I spent most of this time in Luxemburg, and then stayed in France some more and went to England. It was after the war, you see, and while handling the dead, they paid me extra for that. Put 'em in their caskets and sealed 'em up and shipped 'em back for burial here. Come back to the States in 1921. My second enlistment wa'n't over, so they stationed me in a number of places: Fort Dix, Plattsburg, Fort Jay, Camp Travlis, Camp Jackson, Fort Perry, Camp Zachary Taylor, Fort Oglethorpe.

"When I finally did get my discharge, I hit it back here to the hills. And what I've done since coming back is a cue to the world. I've logged and lumbered in about ever' holler in these hills, and I have made whisky, enough to float all them sawlogs out of here. I've been acquainted with three men who was witches and witchdoctors—can do a little witch healing myself. I've been constable two or three times and arrested ever'thing going, about it, from moonshiners to killers. Oh, they hain't nothing going but what I've had some hand in it around here.

"Why, I've worked at ever' job going around a lumber mill. I've worked in the hills cutting trees, have cut logs and run 'em out to the haul road. I've hauled logs out of the hills to the mill, by oxens and mules and by tramroad. I have allas been give up to be the best teamster in the mines or in the woods that ever skinned a mule. I could allas make 'em lay down till their bellies rubbed the ground a-pulling big logs or mining cars."

While I was interviewing Jim Couch at Putney, he was laid off from his mining job at nearby Brookside. He then resolved to quit the mines for good. He traded for a farm in a long branch called Craft Colley in Letcher County. When I made my way up a long graveled road to his door to renew our talks, I found a happy and contented man, with his livestock, corn patches, and vegetable garden. His wife was canning vegetables and drying shuck beans on long strings and pickling corn and cucumbers. A bit later, however, as soon as the corn and truck were taken care of, Jim set out for another job, this time at a sawmill set in Wolfe County. He later went with the mill back to Harlan County—he was keeping his word about quitting the mines. On this visit to Craft Colley I asked him to go into his lumbering experiences in detail.

"Well, it begin when I worked so long for the Intermountain Coal and Lumber Company over there at Putney. Worked for them for nineteen year. Started as a hand stacking lumber. Got to watching the boss measure and grade lumber and worked up to that job. They's a lot to learn about it, more than just building a foundation and throwing up boards. For instance, at this set we're now working out I have twenty-four grades of lumber to sort and stack in the right places. There is three grades for ever' kind of tree they saw, and they cut about all kinds—oak, ash, hickory, sugartree, linn, buckeye, beech. And any other kinds they cut I have to take care of it. But most of the softwood has been cut out of this country. The big companies took it first.

"They're several jobs around a mill set. The timber cutters they usually take contract putting the logs to the bottom of the hill. Somebody else takes contract getting 'em to the skidway of the mill. A skidway man rolls 'em up, washes 'em off and trims the big knots and things offen them, and helps roll 'em on the carriage. The sawyer has the skidway man and the blocksetter level the log up for him so he can make the best cuts and the thinnest slabs and get to the good grain. The blocksetter rides the carriage and watches the sawyer to know how far over to set the log for the inch and two-inch cuts, and the sawyer jams her through the circle saw. They turn the log when she comes back and keep on with it till she is sliced up by the saw. The offbear ketches the slabs and throws 'em in a pile to be carried to the boiler to burn, or to the slabpile, and the good boards he drags over to the roller carriage and shoves 'em down the line. On the line is the cutoff man, and he swings a big whizzing saw over and tips the ends square and cuts out the rotten places and leaves all the boards a certain length—eight, ten, twelve, fourteen foot. One of my men takes 'em from the roller carriage and stacks the prime in a pile on our tram truck and the number one, two, as best he can, after I have trained him a little. And when they change logs— anybody working around a mill soon knows what kind o' wood a board is—he has to keep that separate so we can dump the right kind and grade to the right stack.   When he has the tramcar loaded, another of my men goes up and helps push it down along the lumberyard, and they drap off the stuff at the right stacks. I move up and down the yard with my men, stacking it on the stacks. We have to open-stack it so it can dry even, and I lay my strips even in the stacks so they will look like something when we are done.

"Other little old jobs around a mill are the dustboy who wheels the sawdust out of the pit under the circle saw—if the mill don't have a dust blower. And a big important job is the fireman. He has to drag them slabs up in front of the boiler and chop 'em up to about six-foot lengths and stoke 'em in, mixing a little coal to burn the green stuff. He has to keep her full of water and keep the engine oiled, and if he don't have no shed over him nor no hood on the smokestack, he has to fight the firecoals outten his shirt collar. 'Cause when that saw hits a big three-foot hickory log and starts to tonky-tonking and the belts flop up and down, it just about draws the bowels outten that boiler.

"That's about all they are to my job, I guess. But when the boss goes to selling dry lumber and if he don't know where the right grade is, I have to go out and spot it for him, and most of the time that is part of my job—measuring and loading trucks when they come to buy or haul off to ship it in boxcars. I usually take contract stacking by the thousand, taking care of the men and making my own foundations. But it comes down to a salary most of the time. Now I'm earning ten dollars a day, and that's about as much as I could make on a contract.

"I don't know whether I'd ruther work at a mill or in the mines—have been about the same number of years in both. The mines are hard to stay away from, once you get started, but they are uncertain now and they are dangerous. I was making $18.75 a day—when I worked—last time I was in 'em, before I got laid off and moved over here. But I'm satisfied with my money in timber 'cause it's all above ground. They's danger under the hills. They're what come this leg off.

"The first coal I ever dug was in a little old wagon mines on Bull Creek in Perry County. I was just fourteen year old and got out hunting me a job. I run up on an old feller, and he asked me if I could load coal. I told him I didn't know what loading coal was. He said if I wanted to work, he would learn me. I told him I wanted to work, and he took me on. He run about seven or eight men, and took me in there and give me a shovel. Man alive, that was the hardest work in the world till I got used to it. I had to crawl back in there, and by the time you get to the face of the coal, you are on your hands and knees or you are duck-walking around in there. The shovel was actually a big scoop, and you start on first one knee and then the other, and then you try it on both knees till it's just about a-killing you. And then you come to the only way they are to load a lot o' coal, and that is to set right flat down and stick your legs out as straight as you can, scooping it up and throwing it up in the car with the small of your back. That'll make a man outten you in about a week—or kill you one. You're hunkered down with a heavy carbide lamp on your cap, you're almost shoveling dust and powder smoke right in your own face, and you're breathing that stale foul air and a-straining ever' muscle on your frame. Sweat pops out all over you in a minute, and that bugdust works up into a compound and ever'where you move you are grinding it into your hide. You talk about white-eying on the job—I come in a pea a-doing it on my first job in the mines.

"They hauled the coal out of this mines with mules and took it to the railroad in wagons. That mule job looked good to me. I loaded coal there a week or two, and finally my boss named mule skinning to me. Boy, I grabbed that job before you could stomp your old hat. I thought I was the biggest thing in the world. I'd get hooked up to a car or two of coal, get my whip ready, and crawl on the end of a car and ride out of there and ride back in with empties. That old mule had a heap more sense than I did about the mines. They are rises and down-grades all under the hills. That old mule would run hisself to death on a down grade in order to get 'em over the next rise. He was working in pitch dark, but he knowed the turns and rises better than I did. I worked there for four or five months, I guess, at two dollars a day. That was what he paid his men for working the mines.

"I quit that job because the same man was running some timber, and I worked in the hills for him about nearly a year. Then I got another job in another mines in east Kentucky, a mule mine, too, but they had a tipple built off the hill to the railroad, where the coal was loaded into gons. I went there and hired as a teamster to drive their mules, and they give me a string of three mules, one behind the other, to bring the cars out from under the hill to the dump. I worked at that job nearly a year, quit and left.

"I went back to Harlan country and went to work at the Kellioka Mines. This time I was loading coal again. In mines

they work in groups or crews. They invented a cutting machine—had a big long nose with revolving teeth on it—and that
thing could be drug right up to the face of the coal and right
again' the floor. Start her out and cut under the seam of coal
six or eight feet or more. Another crew come in of a night and
bored holes in the face, put in charges of powder or dynamite,
and shot that room down. Went on to the others all night.
Smoke settled or was drawed out by the ventilation drift by
next morning, and the loaders come in, usually working two
to a room, laid their track up to the face where the coal was
shot down, and loaded it in one, two, five ton cars. Always
loaded it at so much a ton.

"Well, I had a buddy in this mines to help me in my room.
One morning we was in there working, cleaning up a rockfall
where the top had fell in. I went out looking for a bar to
prize with, and when I come back, he was lying there—killed.
Slate fall. Big rock on him that had come down from the top.
That cured me of going under the hill. I tore out of there
and never went back in the mines again for a long time.

"But a man can't stay outten them, seems like. The next
mines I worked in was at Evarts on Bailey's Creek. Another
old mule mines. I worked there a right smart bit and quit to
work for my brother-in-law at Draper. We was going in one
morning with a load of steel tracking loaded behind us. We
was riding in front with two more fellers, both setting right
beside us. The driver run into some timbers with that big
load of steel. I hit the bottom of the car just as flat as I could
get, and one of them steel rails rammed right into the feller
setting next to me and killed him. He was setting right next
to me. I got scared of the mines again and quit and left there.

"I never worked in the mines again for several more years,
but I went back in the mines in 1943. I quit logging and took
a job at Brookside, loading coal with a big new long-wall, a
place where you can get all the way from five to ten cars at a
shooting. Me and my brother was working a room, and I
cleaned up my side of the wall, but he liked [lacked] about a

car or car and a half for a cut when we had to come out. Next morning we went in, and I got down on his side of the wall and was helping him. The top last night was just as sound as it could be. I had got three or four shovelfuls of coal shoveled in the car and stooped back to get me another un, raised up, and here she come. A big rock out of the top about thirteen inches thick come down and covered me up. Got me down. My brother started to run off to get help and leave me, thought I was killed. I hollered at him, told him not to leave me. I was covered with that rock. I knowed my foot was cut off, but besides that, I didn't think I was hurt anywheres else. He come back to me, trying to get me out, and couldn't do much with that big rock. And I told him to get outten there and get enough men in there and get that rock offen me. They come in and finally got me out.

"A little motorman there he hauled me out. My leg had to be taken off. I was out of the mines then for nearly a year. I went back in the same one and found the same man that hauled me out was still there. He come in and pulled my first cars of coal, and then went on to pull another feller's cars right above me. All at once the top fell in on him and killed him. We had to beat the rock offen him and haul him out on top of his own motor.

"Now they are several jobs in the mines that I've not mentioned yet. The track crew keeps up the main line and lays track in the rooms as they are mined out and pull it outten them already worked out. The motorman has a brakesman and coupler who works around the tail end of the load, hooking on, sidetracking cars, pulling the load out of there. Safety crews install fans and test the air gas, and lay down rock dust to keep the bugdust from exploding, and crews on the outside on the tipple screen the coal, wash it, picking out bone and gob. And lots of others in big mines around the machine shop, powerhouse, running the commissary, and all like that.

"I was working down in Jay-main later. Cleaned up my room, me and my buddy name o' Bill Youngblood. We got it

clean and then timbered her up the way we allas done to have
a safe room. The machine come in and cut it and went on to
the other'n. My buddy started to knock out them timbers. And
I told him not to do that. He hammered the top, and it hammered sound. So he knocked that timber out, and down come
a piece from the top, rock about twenty-five feet long, and
killed him.

"I've worked a many a day under the hill when I wa'n't
figuring on getting out alive at night. The top was allas so bad.
When we took out a cut o' coal from our room, we would have
to set up our timbers to hold the top. Set me four cross collars
and timbers under 'em. In a lot of mines they are seams of coal
about six feet above the one you are working, and when you
take out the cut underneath, that six-foot layer of rock between
the seams would come loose—where it was cracked and faulty—
and set right down on your timbers. You would be working
in a death trap all the time, sorter like a deadfall you ketch
animals in. But after that rock had all settled down, it wouldn't
do no more till you took out another cut. As fast as you took
her out, that rock would fall without a sound—if you didn't
have your timbers set. They was holding up all that rock and
the rest of the mountains.

"The weight of the whole ridge above you was wanting to
come down. Why, man, you can hear all kinds of popping and
groaning back in the mines. I've seen my timbers break and
kick out and fly fifteen feet sometimes, so much weight on 'em.
They are all kind of noises in the mines to scare you. You
could hear cracking and grinding all the time. Some of it got
to be imagination. But you get a man in a death trap in under
these old hills, and I reckon he orght to be scared after seeing
so much death and killing."

Jim told of his experiences casually, as if they happened to
men every day. And they do. Lumbering and mining are the
region's chief industries, employing perhaps a hundred thousand men in rough, hard labor. Jim will report on other
folkways of his family in later chapters.

CHAPTER 2

DAVE COUCH, HIS FAMILY STORY

AT TIMES Jim Couch was very elusive on his day (sometimes two days) off in the week. "He don't stay here much on Saturday when he don't work," his teen-age son Elmer would say; "generally takes off sommers and lays out a corn patch or half the garden for me to hoe. I've not got into that corn up yander yit—don't expect to."

And again, "We don't know when he's going to come back in the door when he takes off. He goes down there in that town [Harlan] and stands around joking with ever'body, and he shoots pool all over the place, and then he might wind up in the picture show and not come in till the bus runs at sebem o'clock, or somebody brings him in."

One Saturday, determined to catch Jim, I left Pine Mountain School an hour earlier than I ever had. But they told me he had left "sommers" just a few minutes before and that he might still be down at Harrison's. I did find him on the road at his brother's place, but the two were hustling to go somewhere in a waiting car. I called before they could get moving, "Hello there, Jim; where are you off to today?"

He came up to the car with a wicked smile and his lips pouched out. "What do you say, ole pal? We just can't get together a-tall, seems like. Can't talk any today, have to go on some business with my brother." I don't know how helpless I looked, but I felt let down. He continued, "Get out and talk with my brother Dave. He's here. That's him standing over yander. Dave, come over here—man wants to see you."

A lean man came our way, dressed in baggy pants and some kind of wool coat, pipe in one side of his mouth, heavy-lensed glasses in round metal frames nearly dropping off his nose. A bit taller than Jim, he walked with wide, cautious strides. He came inquiringly in our direction.

Jim continued, "Here's the feller I's telling you about, collecting them old stories and songs. He wants to know can you sing any songs with that banjer. He puts 'em on record."

Dave said "Howdy," took his pipe out, and leaned against the car door. "Why, I used to could sing some of 'em. What ones have you already re-corded?"

Jim and I named a few. Dave said, "I used to play on the banjer some, but I hain't been able in a few years. Eyes got bad and had to retire from work. I'll study some up and get that old banjer in order. Hain't no strings on it now. You let me know when you're coming again—come back in two weeks, a month, and I'll see what I can do for you."

With this uncertain state of affairs I could not arrange a definite time to see him again—he was sure he could not sing any songs for recording until his sore throat got better. But to do all I could to speed the time, I bought a set of banjo strings in town and left them with him on my return that day. He received them with some surprise and, though he didn't say it, perhaps with some obligation to record for me.

Dave lived a mile or so below the mill town of Putney, below the highway and across the railroad tracks, in an average-sized yellow frame house. A few steps from the front porch a rustic bridge spanned a small ravine. The Cumberland River made a long clear sweep on the lower side and had in time cut away a portion of Dave's precious garden. He had built up a high stone wall in front to control the ravine and on the river side to keep the river away. There were fruit trees all about the place, and all around the house were rank cabbages, beets, onions, and other truck. If Dave and the boys wanted to catch any fish from the river, all they had to do was to stand in the garden and cast their hooks over into the rippling water. He had only one neighbor in the long bend of the river.

There was a chill in the air on the riverbank the first part of September when I drove down to Dave's house for our first talk. Two or three dogs greeted me, but there were no people in sight. Some smoke oozed up from the living-room chimney. The noise of my car and the barking of the dogs brought two of the boys, Bige and Birchel, healthy, bright fellows of about sixteen and twelve, to the door. Yes, their father was in the house by the fire, one said, as they left the door open and retired from the threshold. I could now see Dave inside, opposite the warm heating stove in the middle of the small, square room. He was in his lounging chair, taking even puffs on his bent-briar pipe. He asked me to come in, motioning to a couch facing the front of the stove. The evening shadows in the deep valley, aided by the close apple trees in the yard, darkened the room.

We talked for several minutes on current news, Dave becoming talkative, pleasant and hospitable. Of his eleven children, about half of them were grown and married, or off working somewhere. Two small ones, younger than the twelve-year-old boy, ventured into the room on short errands and returned to the dining room, where the mother and two older girls worked with the pots and pans. As my eyes got accustomed to the shadowy interior, I noticed that the house was well kept and had the usual pictures on the walls and a few sentimental posters on religious themes. Several potted plants had been brought indoors and rowed along the wall opposite the couch. To my surprise, I caught sight of a good-looking guitar in another corner of the room. Birchel played around on it, they told me, but he let it sit there unplucked for the time. Bige spoke of a banjo in the bedroom, went for it, and handed it to its rightful picker—the father. Dave complained of his voice and played a few pieces without singing the words.

By this time I was at home. The mother came in with a

lighted oil lamp and set it on a ledge and then retired again. She was strikingly short, with a round face and black hair swept back to a knot at the nape. She was well preserved after mothering eleven. The murmuring stove and simple light cast the right spell for tales. I asked Dave if he was ready to tell a few. His silence heightened the spell of magic in the room; the smaller two children left their play on the floor and went to his chair.

"Oh, I'll tell one so's these little fellers'll go to bed."

The older children grew quiet and respectful, while the smaller two mulled over the ones they would like to hear. The youngest boy named one that just suited him. It was for children, the cumulative type, with its simple formula and constant repetition. The other voices became silent when the father began testing his vocal cords. He slid his pipe down his coat and into the pocket and told the story of the Cat and Rat [microcard ed., No. 31]. The children went off to bed.

For the remainder of that session and in many more that followed, I asked Dave questions about his home life and listened to his stories and songs. He liked to tell of his early days, lingering over some with pleasure and others with something like tears in his voice.

"I lived a life on a farm," Dave began, "up till I was grown, till I was about seventeen. My father had to farm purty heavy to make a living for us ten chillren, and he had to make everything except what we had to buy, such as coffee, sugar, salt, hardware, and things like that. We would go to the fields come spring and raise our corn, beans, 'taters. And when winter come, we had to go in purty times and bring in our fodder stacks and pull our corn and get it in to the barn. We had five cows to milk, eighteen or twenty head of hogs to feed, chickens, geese, ducks. But still I think we had a easier time of it than what people have now. Now most of the time people go to the store and buy what they can get. They have to get out and work it out, and then get out and pack it in. I'd take old times now again.

"We lived in a big log house, had two sixteen-foot rooms, with two porches, one on each end. The dogtrot between these two rooms was covered over and made a good place to store up things like plowstocks, feed, and wood for the fires. As for gyarden truck, we didn't have cans to can things back then. We would hole up nearly everything we raised, such as turnips, 'taters, cabbage, apples—even hole up our beets. Take our beets up when we needed 'em on the table and pickle 'em fresh. We would have enough fresh cabbage and stuff in them holes to last us till growing season the next spring, and I think that was a purty good living. I'll tell ye what all we would put up other ways. We would pickle up a sixty-two-gallon barrel full of beans, my mother would. And she had a fifty-five-gallon barrel she would put up full of roas'in' years, and kraut a fifty-gallon barrel full of kraut. When the heavy frostes come, we would get out and kill about eight hogs, put up sausage and meat and lard. Milk them five cows and have plenty of meat, milk, and butter. We lived a purty good life back in them days.

"Now we would do more with beans than just pickle 'em. We would dry a sight of beans by stringing them and threading them up on strings to dry. I've knowed my mother to dry as many as eighteen bushel thrashed out for soup beans. We boys would get them right real dry, and take and put them in sacks, get us some big sticks, and go to work. I've beat 'em out a many a time that way, going atter 'em just like killing snakes, bust them hulls up, take them out on a sheet or something, and sort the beans out of the hulls. We called these shelly beans.

"For our clothing we had sheep. We raised our sheep in the old fields and sheared 'em in the summertime and sent the wool off to have it wove into cloth to make clothes out of. We'd give half of the wool to the company to send us the weaving of the rest of it in jeans cloth. We allas had plenty of clothing but it wa'n't so nice—you know how jeans clothes would look. It wa'n't striped or colored, nothing like that, but still it was warm and comfortable, and we didn't mind the looks of it. Out of that jeans my mother would make our pants, shirts, and everything we wore excepting our shoes. We would get one pair of shoes a year, the fall of the year—brogans—and they had to last till time to go barefooted again. My mother would spin some for her own use. She would make yarn, and knit our socks, jackets, gloves, and toques for our heads.

"I remember one summer we had in a big crop and my father got down with the sore-eye. He had taken it and went nearly blind till he couldn't see and left everything to do, with just me and my mother and the other littler uns. We pitched into that work and got the crop laid by, and then we needed money, so we sanged in the woods and got money to buy our shoes and things we had to have in the winter we couldn't get no other way. I was just nine year old, and that was the first time I recollect going out sanging. I learnt to sang because my mother didn't have nobody to go with her. I went along to keep her company and to carry the sang. But in a couple or three days I learnt what sang was, and I went to digging it. I dug about half what she would, and I felt proud because I was helping out a little. I've been a-sanging ever since. I guess I've dug and sold $10,000.00 worth, if not more. It sold about five dollars a pound back when we first begin to dig it, and it has raised to about fifteen dollars now. I made $798.00 summer before last sanging and digging ginger. Last summer I was sick all the time and didn't get to sang none, and I hain't getting to sang any this summer. Maybe I'll get all right and sang some this fall. I'd ruther sang in the fall. You'll find as much sang in the spring before all the weeds come as you will in the fall, but it'll dry away half in the spring, but it won't dry away any to amount to nothing in the fall. You can see it all right in the spring, in the summer you've got to get in under the weeds, but in the fall you can see its big pod of red berries sticking up and it commences getting yaller and you can see about all of it.

"My mother would start her spinning on her wheel early enough in the fall to have yarn for us a pair of socks around before it got cold. Then later she would get time and spin all

of her yarn and knit the other need-cessities. We got two pair
of socks a year. My younger sisters didn't learn how to run the
wheel, but they hope [helped] Mother with the wool and they
could knit, help her run off socks, gloves—a pair a year—and
they'd knit 'boggans or toques to wear on our heads, and
sweaters, and my mother used to knit shawls for the women to
put around 'em when it was cold. She would color that yarn.
Mother had about three colors she would generally prepare.
She'd take warnut roots, skin the bark off, boil it, and make
yaller color. Take chestnut-oak roots and make a dye out of it,
but it was about the same color warnut was. She would take
mulberry roots and make another color, on a yaller color but
more darker. Other dyes she got from her neighbors or the
store, or ordered it from a company.

"The first salt I remember seeing I was about eight year old.
My father he went to Goose Creek on a sebem-day journey
going and coming to get our salt. And I want to tell you while
I'm into it what he hauled it on. I guess it'll sus-prise you. He
had a big cart, and he made it hisself. He made the axles out of
hickory, well seasoned, and he made his wheels out of blackgum,
the toughest wood in the world, wood that wouldn't split. You
could split it one way as good as you could the other. He sawed
off big solid cuts offen that blackgum, about twenty inches in
diameter, with big auger holes in the center for his axles, and
pagged on. Never had a nail then and weren't a nail in the
whole wagon. Made a bed for it and a tongue and doubletrees
for his oxen. Oxen had double yokes on 'em, and the leaders
would have a big chain hooked to a swivel in the yoke of the
ones behind.

"His wagon was pulled by two yoke of oxens and he would
be gone from sebem to nine days. He would go out and get a
load and divide it out with his neighbors, and then they would
go for one when that run low. He would bring back about two
thousand, three thousand pounds of it, bring back a big load
in about one-bushel sacks. It didn't cost more'n about fifty
cents a hundred, but that trip cost more than the price again'

they got it back home. That was the only way to get salt, go
to the works over there where they 'vaporated it in kittles.
No railroads in this country back then.

"The first load of goods I ever saw come into that country
was hauled by Will Morgan. He had to haul from Hagan,
Virginia. No railroad closter. The first log wagon I ever seen
come into the Greasy country was one with sebem yoke of
steers to it and one pair of mules. The mules was leading the
wagon.

"Coffee that we'd have was bought at the clostest place, and
we would generally buy it in fifty-pound sacks of green grains.
We had to parch it and then grind it; my mother had that to
do every morning for breakfast. Them fifty pounds would last
us about six months, and sacks of sugar would be brought in at
the same time, fall, so we wouldn't have it to do in the winter.

"Now they had watermills to grind their meal, after we quit
grinding or gritting it at home. My father had a big watermill
over in the Sang Branch where we lived. When it would start
into raining in the fall, we would get busy and grind up our
corn to make our bread through the winter and up till summer.
And we had to have a certain way of putting it up to keep it
from sp'iling. We'd have coaloil barrels made out of staves
that helt about fifty-five gallons. Most of them barrels never had
coaloil in 'em, but we just called all barrels that, I reckon.
We'd put our meal in 'em this way. Put in about two bushel
and then put in a layer of salt to hold the meal from sp'iling,
and then put in another two bushel and another layer of salt.
Several barrel was supposed to last us till up in the summer,
when our corn come in and we had water to grind more. We
had to put up everything that way to do us.

"We didn't raise no wheat. We didn't have no biscuits in
the house till after I was grown, and then we had so fer to go
to get groceries like that we didn't have no biscuits except on
Sunday for breakfast. The railroad finally come through to
Pineville and later up the river to the Pore Fork. Still it was
about twenty-sebem mile from where we lived. We would start

out from home on mules on a Sunday morning, over the Pine Mountain, and get to the store here at night. Stay all night, and early Monday morning we would load up with flour and stuff and head back acrost the mountain for home. We didn't eat flour like people do now sebem days a week. We had cornbread three times a day. But it was good. It was baked this way. We had a big farplace where my mother cooked, and she had a big baker and led [lid]. They was ten of us chillern, and she had to bake a lot. She would fill that thing full of dough, draw out the farcoals and make a place to set it, put it in the hot ashes, and put that led on and then cover it plumb over with hot coals. It come out of there brown all over, and it was the best bread you ever eat, and if you hain't eat none of it, you've missed something. Put it in that far and let it bake, and pull her out of there and eat. Man, oh, man, you don't know how good that is. Take butter and good ham meat—awful good. I wish times would come back just like they was back then.

"We would hunt all the spare time we had. Didn't have much hunting time in the summer, but in the winter we would hunt possums, groundhogs, coons, things like that. No big game in that country. Of a winter we'd catch, oh, eighty, hundred hides and ship 'em off or sell to some buyer. We done a lot o' squirrel hunting, and we could get a mess ever' time we went out. Used an old hog rifle most of the time. The first squirrel I ever kilt was with one of them. Me and my brother—I was only thirteen and he was elebem—we started out one morning with our squirrel dog, and I took along the old shotgun because I had two shells fer it. Got two squirrels and come back. Looked over the old hog rifle and saw I had just fourteen caps and some powder. So I took my bullet molds and molded me fourteen bullets. Me and him started out again that evening, about a mile above where we live, up a holler. The dog treed one, and I kilt it. He went on and treed again, and I shot that un out. Jim was coming along carrying 'em. First thing I knowed, we had thirteen squirrels and started out to the house. The dog treed another un up a small tree. Hit was setting up there looking at me, and I raised up to aim with the last load I had. I went to far on that squirrel, and the cap dropped off. I couldn't find it. Back then we had old redheaded matches. You could lay one on a rock and bust it, and it would go like a dynamite cap. I cut me off a head from one of them matches and put it on the tube of my gun and let her go and killed that un. Made me sixteen squirrels I kilt that day.

"Well, we got to school part of the time. Our school was four mile from where we lived. While I was small, I didn't get to go because it was too fer, but time I's thirteen, I went every day I could, three, four days a week if it wa'n't bad. We'd go most of the time to get to play, had games at school, play and throw rocks going and coming. Be tard playing and running all day and wouldn't get home till near dark, and we would have to get in wood and kindling, do up the work, feed the stock.

"I'd study my lessons of a night so I'd know 'em the next day and get to play all I could. We had some old books, called readers then, from the primer to sebemth, eighth readers. I went through the fourth reader, was as fer as I got. When I was eighteen, going on nineteen, my mother died, and I never got to go to school any more. My father then he broke up housekeeping, and we went to live with the neighbors and kinfolks. I went to stay with my brother on Gabe's Branch on Greasy. Stayed there and worked for him and got to making whisky. While my mother was living, I never made no moonshine, for she wouldn't let me. She made us go to church on Sunday, and she wanted us around close through the week where she could keep in touch with us, afeared we might get into something another. After she died and left us, then our father he didn't take too good a care of us. He just about turned us out, or else we just left. I had a living to make for myself. Got into whisky making and bootlagging. Thought I's having a good time, but I wa'n't. I just wa'n't satisfied the reason I done that. I didn't have no mother to go to, and I had to have some place to stay. And I got so I'd just as soon be in the hills at a still as at somebody's house.

"The lastenest thing I can remember at school was the teacher's thrashing and whupping us. The last year I went to school I was a big man—thought myself a man. And this last year I taken a whuppin' offen a teacher, but the teacher took one, too. I fit the old feller. When he'd hit me, I'd hit him. It was over fighting. Me and some boys got into a fight. He wanted to whup me and leave them out. I told him if he didn't whup them, I wa'n't aiming to take my whuppin'. It made him mad, and he said he's going to whup me anyhow. He got a-holt of me and went to thrashing me, and I went to fighting him back, and me and him just fit it out. He whupped me all right, cut the blood outten me, but I kicked his shins and skinned 'em all over. He told my dad and said if I didn't come back to school, he's aiming to have me sunt off. Dad sunt him back word that if he'd treat us all alike, they wouldn't 'a' been no fight of it. Whup me and the other boys and give it to all the chillern when they needed it. And the old man was right. The teacher wanted to whup me, and I didn't think it was right.

"Well, we would play ball and base and other games. The ball game was about like baseball. We would get thirty minutes for morning recess, an hour at dinner, and a half an hour for evening recess. And we'd play after school till we had to go home. I took many a whuppin' for coming in late, but I liked to play. On Sunday we'd go to church and take all day for it. We'd play with our friend boys till dark, just about it. Get in home to do the work so that on Monday we could hit the fields. Spring we went to grubbing and getting the ground in shape, plant the corn and go to hoeing it, and work every day till it was laid by.

"When the crops come in, we'd have to start gathering 'em and putting 'em up. When our beans come in, we'd have bean stringings. Many of a time I've gone to the field with my mother to pick sacks of beans. You understand, beans then hain't like they are now; we could pick three, four times as many offen a row then. No bugs then, and we had big rich fields. I've picked many a three-bushel meal sack offen a row.

Pick till dinnertime, and our father would come and help carry them beans in. Pick twenty bushel in the day. Then they would let us all tell our neighbors to come in for a bean stringing. Father and mother would tell us if we got them beans strung and not waste any, we could play the rest of the night. Sometimes it would be two o'clock in the morning when we got 'em worked up and threaded on strings and broke up for pickling, but we worked patiently till we'd git 'em finished on account o' getting to play all we could. We would have six or sebem bean stringings a season.

"Then we would start playing. I allas played the banjer for the sets and never did get to run any sets, but I've played for many a set to be run. Some would have to wait—couldn't get in the set—and they'd stand back and clap their hands to keep up the movement. When they would get tired, they'd play quiet games like Pleased or Displeased. They danced a lot, and they would get me to pick. I played for sets from the time I was twelve year old. If I didn't get to run many with 'em, I got a big kick outten playing the banjer for 'em.

"They would play in the house all the time. Back then people was kindly curious about letting a big gang bunch up outside. If they got to running in and out and carrying on, they would have to go home. I've been to places where they had jugs of whisky out in the weeds to run to, but at home and while my mother was alive, she wouldn't have no jugs of whisky at our parties. She was a Christian—from the time I can recollect till she died, she was a Christian. She would get down on her knees and pray by her bedside of a night. I've heared her pray for her sick chillern many of a time. The sweetest prayers I ever heared pray was from the lips of my mother.

"We had other parties when there was other things going on in the neighborhood. We'd raise cane and have molasses all the time. Everybody raised cane. We would have a stir-off every night when we got to making 'lasses. Get the cane into the mill and grind it into juice of a day, and then it would take us till sometimes two o'clock in the night to get it stirred off.

Then we would carry the molasses in and get everything cleaned
up for the next night. We would have some of the same games
we had at the other get-togethers. Run sets, play Pleased or
Displeased, or Old Dock Jones, London Bridge. I don't know
how many different games they would play, but a lot of them.
The sets was about like them they have here today. I didn't
call any and didn't learn 'em. I played the banjer all the time,
'cause they wa'n't just anybody who could play one. Had to
play fast for the dances. When they would start, somebody
would call it, and all could get in went round with 'em while
others stood out and clapped. They would be making so much
noise with their hands and feet you couldn't hear nothing.
Had to play the banjer loud.

"Old Dock Jones was just a circle game:

> Old Dock Jones was a fine old man,
> He told a thousand lies,
> Gentlemen and ladies sail away.

They would go round and round, you see, getting faster and
faster all the time. They would be one in the middle, and the
others would say, 'Kiss whoever you please.' The one in the
middle would kiss one that was in the ring, and the one kissed
would have to go in the middle and let that one take his place
in the set.

"In London Bridge two would hold their hands up, you
know, like a bridge, and they would go around atwixt them
under their arms and say

> The London Bridge is a-fallin' down,
> Fallin' down, fallin' down—

and finally it would fall down and catch one. That's the way
they played it.

"Now in Pleased or Displeased they would all set down in a
line, and they took it in rotation. Commence with the first one
and say, 'Pleased or displeased?' 'Displeased.' 'What would it
take to please you better?' You could make any wish you

wanted to to the crowd, you see. Maybe it would be for one
to go bark up the chimbly, or kneel down and pray, or whatever you put on him to do he had to do it. Make 'em go wade
the water, bring in a load o' wood for the far, bring you a drink,
stand on their head. But most of the time it was hugging and
kissing. Say it would please you to see some boy hug a purty
girl, or some girl kiss a purty boy, you know, getting all the fun
outten it you could. Sometimes some smart boy would want
you to go pick up a rock and pack it a piece and lay it down, or
go rub farcoals on your face and make your face black. Anything to get a good un on somebody.

   "We went to church every Sunday. Didn't have any meetings
of a night like they do now. We had church about all day Sunday. Commence about ten o'clock, have four, five preachers
going on till late dinnertime. Sometimes we had dinner on
the ground. And when we didn't, we would go home with
somebody who wanted to set a big dinner at the house. That
day then and this day now is different. That day then you could
get a meal anywhere just by going home with a crowd of the
meeting folks. Fifty people eating at the table of their neighbor
was a small thing then. I've seen fifty eat at our house a many
of a time, and up in fifty. When they took dinner to church,
they would bake up fruit cake and sweetbread, and fill baskets
with pies and chicken and take to the meeting, and when they
finally called a recess, hour maybe, we would all eat and go
back to preaching. Maybe it would be a baptising or decorating
the graves. The evening meeting would break up about three
o'clock, and all would go home. They would be five or six
preachers and would all preach, give 'em all a chance, and
sometimes one would preach an hour, maybe two hour. Get
them old Baptists started, Hardshell Baptists, into it, and they
wouldn't know when to quit. They was a few other denomina-
tions, but most of the old people were Hardshell Baptist. We
would sing them old songs by lining 'em out. I learnt many of
them, and I've heared my father and mother sing 'em all day.

   "One of the best times for my mother to tell us them old

stories was when dad would be out and couldn't get back in till late. My mother would have the grub ready, but we would have to wait till he come, even if it was 'way in the night. And to keep us pacified, she would tell tales. Dad would not get to work often, and when he did, it would be eight, ten mile from home. He would work till dark and then come in home so we could all set to the table and eat together and go to bed. Mother would tell us a tale, and if he hadn't come in, we would want another un, and she would be willing to go on telling. When he come, mother would set down and let one of the girls wait the table. She would turn thanks, and then she retch the food and broke bread for the chillern and got us all started eating. My father wa'n't a Christian till my mother died, he never went to church much till after she died, but my mother made it a Christian home.

"We all had a good time, got along good; they wa'n't no quarreling in the family like they is today. We all hung together, and when one started to the field, we knowed what to do. We all knowed where to hang our hoes and where they was next morning. When one hollered for us in the morning, we knowed to get up and go to the field. When our father told us it was quit time, we would all quit. We'd never bag him to quit like chillern do now. We never had much sickness in the home till my mother died. I had a brother to die. The next to the oldest one, he took epilepsy fits and kindly lost his mind, and we sent him off to Lexington. He died and is buried there. And I had another brother died accidentally. Feller let a gun go off, and it killed him. But we never had much sickness like people do now.

"My father used all the signs in his planting. He planted corn and beans when the sign's in the arms; 'taters when the sign was in the feet; sowed his cabbage and things like that growed heads when the sign was in the head; planted all his vines when the sign was in the secrets. We allas raised plenty of stuff and never did fail. They's three days of the year, called barren days, when he wouldn't plant anything. We allas tended fifteen to twenty acres of corn every year, sowed hay and mowed it. We had stock and had to raise food for it. We would kill our hogs all the time on the old of the moon. Never would kill 'em on the new of the moon on account of the meat being tough and we wouldn't get as much lard out of it on the new of the moon as we would on the old of the moon. The old people could tell about when it was going to rain by the wind or clouds. My father could look at the clouds or watch the wind of an evening, and when he would say it would rain by morning, it generally rained. People went by the signs then more than they do by the almanac now. They didn't have almanacs then, and it was mostly their signs that they went by. We could tell what time it was by the sunset, you see. We had a sun mark to tell when twelve o'clock come. When we was in the field and our shadders slipped right up under us, we knowed it was about dinnertime. About quit time we would watch the sun on the other side of the mountain, and when it got to what looked like about six inches from the top, we went out. It was about dark.

"Another thing that we done with food back then I don't hear mentioned anymore was the way we handled our berries. We would dry our berries just the way we dried apples, and then put 'em away in something tight. Get them out in the wintertime when you get ready to cook 'em. Put them in water, and they would be just like fresh from the vines. We picked a lot of huckleberries along the tops of the ridges and dried them. Man, they was good in pies along about Christmastime. Some people dried their blackberries that way.

"I begun making moonshine back before my mother died, but she bagged me not to make. I quit and went to Pine Mountain School to work and stayed with my oldest brother who lived on Gabe's Branch about five mile from the school. I worked for the school for about thirteen months for seventy-five cents a day, and I paid my brother twenty-five cents for board. After working there for about a year, year and a half, why, my mother died. She had cancer in her left breast. She passed away at the age of sixty-four years old. My father sold about all we had, except what my mother give the chillern before she died."

The next years of his life, Dave's main occupation was making moonshine, although he worked for a time on the railroad near Hazard and again at a mine on Bailey's Creek. "But they's not much more for me to tell. After that I got a job at Lynch working on the railroad. Worked some more at Bailey's Creek. And then for eighteen year I worked for the Intermountain Coal and Lumber Company. That was on Pore Fork at Putney. There's where I live now. I'm fifty-five year old, going on fifty-six. I hain't worked nowheres in two year. I've been under medical treatment and in the hospital. Had a operation two year ago and haven't worked any since. That's brought you up to right now, and I guess that's about all that I can recall at this time."

CHAPTER 3

OTHER COUCHES, THEIR STORIES

MANDY HENDRIX, older sister of Dave and Jim Couch, still lived in an isolated valley on the northeast slope of the Pine Mountain. She was the first member of the family that I met, and although she never told me any folktales, it was she who directed me to Jim at Putney. My experiences on the trip that discovered her are among the highlights of my life as a folklore collector.

Miss Grace Rood, the field nurse for the hospital of the Pine Mountain School, invited me to go with her to the Cutshin valley. We went down Greasy, up Big Laurel, and over a very rugged ridge, and came out on the gap between Big Leatherwood and Cutshin. Miss Rood was driving her tried and trusted four-wheel-drive jeep—and we needed it. We dropped down the lane of a small mining camp in the gap, passing cabins on stilts along the woods on either side.

At the end of the row the muddy road became an unimproved trail in the rocks and branch water of Cutshin. We bounced along in the bed of the small ravine, here taking a rutted highroad over a ledge and there plunging into the water again. The little streams were swollen with recent rains and continued to add their volume to the main creek. Soon we were fording Cutshin endways, with not a single foot of highroad left. Rocks and driftwood became the main hazard as we navigated the rushing, roiling stream. The water was soon lapping the bottom of the vehicle and seeping through the holes in the floor. Unexpected boulders about the size of number-seven washtubs tossed the tires up into view and let them fall again into the fresh mountain water. I could only grip the iron bars of my seat and trust to the instinct of the driver. She could see no more road than I could. As the water became deeper, I was afraid for our safety. The hills were higher because we were lower in the trough of two steep mountain slopes. The thickets of rhododendron and mountain laurel came down to the rocks that lined the canyon. Although I had been in the hills of Kentucky most of my life, I believed this to be the wildest and most untouched section that I had seen.

At last a house appeared. It was not much, but it was a house, the kind people live in through the hills. It was a log building with a porch, a paling fence around it and the garden patch, a shed for the old bony cow, and washtubs beside the little ravine that gurgled down to join the main creek. It was a sight to lift sagging spirits. Just below the house the road rose to a notch in the hill and wound along above the roiling waters.

Still farther on we came to the mouth of an apparently rather long creek, judging from the volume of water issuing across the road. Right in the mouth of the valley was a vast oblong rock fifty feet long, almost blocking the valley. Our jeep chugged around the base of the rock and under one long ledge, into a pretty mountain dale. There, as if hidden from the world, was a large white store, and to the left beside the stream was a white dwelling house. Horses were hitched to the rail beside the store, where a knot of men talked until they had to step aside to let us pull into the level yard and stop. The storekeeper, a youngish man with ruddy face and pleasant manners, came out and called Miss Rood by name. I spoke of stories and tellers. He said, "Come right on in and make yourselves at home. My mother lives here with us, and she knows about everybody in here and maybe some stories. If she don't know any, she knows who does."

A little old lady sat in a rocker before the open grate and clicked a pair of knitting needles in her small delicate fingers.

Her gray hair was pulled back and tied in a ball at the nape. She had a bit of fire to take the chill and dampness out of the house. We were received with the most warmhearted welcome that one can experience.

I asked about Jack stories, fairy tales, and witch legends. Her face lighted up, and she chuckled in spite of herself. "I know just the kind you are looking fer. It's them old-fashioned fireside stories. Many's the time I set and listened to them when I was growing up. But I'm no hand to tell stories—the way they are likely to be told. No," she said regretfully, "I never was any hand to tell them old-fashioned tales, but used to I'd druther hear somebody come in and tell stories of a night than to eat. I've set and listened to 'em, and ghost tales, they allas come last and would make us little uns so scared we would be afraid to go in the back room to bed.

"Now let me sorter study." She clicked her needles for a minute and mumbled a few names under her breath. And then she told us of a person who could tell them the best in the long ago, but she was not sure the woman followed storytelling any more. I pursued her for the name. "She is Mandy Hendrix, down here on Cutshin. She used to tell them stories while her chillern were growing, but I hain't heared much about her and her stories for years now. She used to be the best un I know of in here now."

Mandy's house lay farther down the Cutshin road and up the first hollow to the right. We stayed with the notch above the stream for three miles, passed through a beech grove whose old worn roots tossed the jeep to and fro, and finally came again to the creek, now a fairly raging flood. On the other side was a steep incline, almost running with mud because a new road was being graded up the valley. Above the fill of mud was a very steep ascent into Guthers Branch, where Mandy lived.

The water rose up under the seat and rolled away from us in muddy waves. The tires spun and threw sand behind as we cut our way up the hill and finally leveled off in a sandy trail untouched by recent travel. Below the first house we ran into a child's sand castle with battlements and stickweed flagpoles. The valley as usual widened out and stretched onward into the towering hills. We took the left branch, along the slick rocks in the roadbed, until the trail twisted up another incline and wound around to the very yard of a house. A model mountain cabin, it was made of small unhewn logs, daubed with yellow clay and covered with rived boards from a clear water oak. Vines ran up at the corners and almost covered the small-paned windows. Flowers were everywhere—in little rows along the graveled walk leading to the plank door, beside the house, and in old automobile tires about the front yard. A pole shed-and-barn stood above the humble dwelling. The hills rose steep and rugged on all sides. Out in the ravine was the family spring, with the customary washkettle and tubs beside it.

A tall lean man of about sixty-five years appeared in the doorway and walked with a game leg out toward the jeep. His faded chambray shirt sagged, and his brown jeans pants hung low on his hipless frame and dropped from broad suspenders. His blond arms and face were mottled with spots of pink and tan.

"Well, if it hain't Miss Rood, 'way up here in this lost holler. Get out, you fellers, and come on in to the house. Who's that with you, Miss Rood? Bring him and come on in where you can set a spell."

This kind and unreserved hospitality, known in my early years, came back to me again and hit me with a sharp delight. It is surely the choice virtue of the Appalachian people. Needless to say, we went in the direction of the house as if drawn by enchantment. Two little boys met us on the way, one about six and the other perhaps twelve, the small one still a chubby child, the other, wearing threadbare overalls and a flop-bill cap, bashful and lean and sad looking. Inside the door sat the woman of the house, close to the fire, her knees almost touching the jambrock. She had an old cloth under her chin and tied at the top of her head over sandy silvery hair brushed back and caught with hairpins. With some effort she rose and made way for us to enter, setting out her chair and drawing another from the back part of the room. "Take this chear, Miss Rood. Set down. I'm ailing," she was saying, "and hain't been able to do a lick o' work for several days," pulling her hair back and smoothing down her long, sacklike dress. "I've got a risin' in my year, and hit's about to kill me. Maybe you can doctor me a little."

Upon entering, I saw that the small cozy sitting room was carefully swept, the wrinkles had been patted out of the feather ticks on the three small beds in the corners, and the garments were hung around the walls. The inside of the room was a typical mountain interior. The walls, ceiling, and even the door facings had been spring-papered with catalog and magazine leaves; the fireboard [mantel] was covered with precious objects such as bottles of medicine and boxes of salve, a kerosene lamp, and the Bible; the beds were covered with handmade crazy quilts; and an old table in the center of the room had its crocheted centerpiece, as did the ledge of the fireboard.

The smaller boy was Mandy's grandson by a daughter who lived farther up the ravine; the older boy, Bobby, was an orphan she had taken to raise when he was three years old. "Hit's a good child and hain't nary bit of trouble to me," Mandy said. "My seven chillern growed up and married off, and I found this un over on Leatherwood. I was glad to give it a home"—then regretfully—"but hit hain't had no schoolin'. Hit's so fer out of here I hain't been able to send it nary day. I wush it could go to school."

After a few more words about the distance from school—five miles down on Cutshin—Mandy continued, "Hit could 'a' gone back to Leatherwood when it was six and maybe 'a' went some, but it didn't want to go, did you, Bobby? I tried to get some of his people to keep him just for the schoolin'. Hit's a McDaniel, and its family broke up and scattered when it was just a sit-alone baby. Hits mother had to be sunt off, and its daddy never tried to keep house anymore. I took hit to raise, and it's been satisfied with me ever since. Don't want to go to its own people

to live. I counsel and teach him all I know, just as I tried to counsel and teach my own houseful of young uns. He minds me and does all the little jobs fer me. I am good to him, maybe better to him than I was to some of my own chillern."

The boy sat with his hands pressed between his knees, his head down, and his eyes hid by the long cap bill, not talking while he was being talked about. But a few minutes later when I had mentioned collecting stories, his head came up, his eyes lighted, and he was speaking about stories he knew, telling lines of the boy up the bean tree [microcard ed., No. 1]. I recognized the authentic oral pattern and turned to Mandy for comment. She said, "We used to tell stories when I was growing up, but I guess my brother Jim is 'bout the only one that tells 'em any more."

"Where did you hear that one, Bobby?" I asked.

"I guess I heared it from Jim, when he used to come over here."

"Brother Jim used to come over and stay with me," Mandy continued, "and ever' night he'd set here and tell stories. He'd have this house full of chillern. They'd be all around him and on both knees. Hit'd pleasure the chillern to death everwhen he come over here. We heared all kinds of stories from our mother, and Jim learnt most of them. After I's married, he stayed with me till he was grown and went off to the World War."

"Mandy, will you tell some of the stories to me?" I asked her. "Your mother seems to have handed down a lot of fine old stories to you children."

"She did hand down a heap o' stories, but I never was no hand to tell 'em. You'll have to look up brother Jim. He lives over there on the river at Putney. He knows more stories than I do and has follered telling 'em. I hain't never told them old fireside tales since my chillern was little."

Not wishing to be put off if it could be avoided, I continued reviewing stories they knew and learned that they had heard their parents tell a great store of tales. Finally I asked her again, only to hear her say, "I've quit telling stories. I've been a Christian for nineteen year and don't tell any more of them big tales. Any more I allas tell the truth."

If this did put a stop to my requests, it was not a new excuse to me. I had heard it from many women and a few men. In the hills the women had begun to equate stories with lies and with obscene yarns not told in mixed company. Mandy's mother years before would not tell stories in the presence of visitors. The ballads had been fading out of tradition for a generation or two. They had come to be called "love ballets" or "devil's ditties," and had begun to die on the lips of the folk, even before the phonograph and the radio inundated them.

The trip was not in vain, of course. Mandy had set me on a trail that I was to follow for the next four years, trying to collect all of those stories handed down by the mother. Even Mandy wanted to help, for at the end of my sessions with all of the family, she promised Jim she would go over all the stories with us to see if she knew of any still uncollected. We did just that, but she was unable by that time to contribute. Also the boy Bobby told interesting versions of two long tales. But above all, I was now on the quest for Jim, the man who could "pleasure chillern to death" with his stories.

For most of these next four years I was a frequent visitor at Jim's house. Since Dave didn't have electricity, it was necessary for me to drive him and others to Jim's home for many sessions of family reminiscences, songs, and tales on the tape recorder.

Early in my quest I wanted to see the father of these folk, the champion banjo picker of the country a generation ago, Tom Couch, who lived on the hill above Jim's house. "And after you get him to talking," Jim warned, "he'll tell you a-plenty. I can't get up and down that hill very good, but you take Elmer to show you the way and go on."

We went up a zig-zag path until we struck a notch carved in the hillside (an old tramroad across Pine Mountain), and around it, passing through groves of shrubbery and by a coal-bank in the hill. The water was dammed up—where the old man got his water, Elmer said. After a few more turns under strips of trees, we came to an open flat, in the middle of which stood an ancient cabin. It was a rude plank box with rougher planks over the cracks, surrounded by a broken hedge of shrubs, wild bushes, flowers, old rose stools; the roof was of tarpaper, almost flat, with a stovepipe jutting out the back side—this was the homeseat of the old man after the spacious home life described and idolized by Jim and Dave! The inmates of the cabin, warned of our approach by the barking of an old shaggy dog, poured out—a boy perhaps twelve, a girl about fourteen, and a long-haired, black-eyed woman of about forty years. Elmer, telling them we had come to hear Grandpa Tom tell big tales, set the boy off in a run up the path calling wildly, "Dad, Dad. Some men want to see you." Old Grandpa Tom was up in the woods cutting wood and rolling down chunks for the fires. Here he came dragging poles in each hand, and at the edge of the notch he dropped them and worked his way out to the ten-foot drop. To my warning him away from the high bank he replied with a fuss full of fiery pride, and taking sprouts in hand, he worked over the edge and landed like a cat at my feet. He was the spriest man of ninety-two I had seen in the hills. Except for the constant and disconcerting tremble of his hands and a red lawless growth on his high cheekbone, he was well preserved.

He had me sit with him in the doorway, although the interior of the cabin was sizzling hot. Within were two beds, a round heater, and a cast-iron cookstove. The boy sat on the doorsill at his father's feet, constantly interrupting the old man. Tom tried to make him mind his manners—"Hush, hush! I want you to hush so I can talk with this man"—batting the wind with his hand.

His people had always lived in the hills of Kentucky, Tom insisted, ignoring or suppressing his probable French origin. One of his forebears started the tradition of picking and singing by making himself a banjo from an old gourd. Sometime in his young manhood Tom took an interest in the banjo and became a contender for prizes at Fourth of July celebrations and in other contests. He related some of his early experiences as if they had happened only yesterday.

"I was down in Hyten [Hyden, seat of Leslie County] when they 'rested me for packin' moonshine, but, the Lord, I never had more 'n that much in a lettle old half-pint bottle," he protested, measuring a few inches with his trembling fingers. "Was in there a week or two—a stranger, ye see, and didn't have nobody to go my bail. Le's see, I believe I had my banjer with me, leastways I could whup on one purty good at that time. I heared they was going to have a banjer contest in town and bagged awful hard to get out and get in that contest. After so long the jailer saw his way to take me out and take me up there. I played as hard as I could and I's playing with the best of 'em. I won third place. I'll tell ye what I played to win. I played Rovin' Gambler [microcard ed., No. 16]. The jedge of the contest come around and put a dollar and fifteen cents in my hand!"

Tom kept the banjo ringing for fifty years, picking up songs as he went about, bringing them home and handing them down to his children. His hearing had begun to deteriorate by this time, and as a consequence, he could no longer stay on pitch. But in the years that followed, Jim went to him often to get the full versions of songs, and once when I went with him, old Tom added a stanza to a song. Finally, toward the end of my collecting, there were two songs that neither Jim nor Dave knew fully, and the only hope again was the old man. Jim also wished that the family could have some record of Tom's singing, no matter how poor it had become. Accordingly, Jim had him come to the tape recorder, into which he sang our only complete versions of I Saw a Sight and Hiram Hubbard [microcard ed., Nos. 36 and 32].

Tom was not a good informant in the folktale, having left this field to his first wife and the boys. Apparently he had heard many of the family stories often; he named several that were familiar to him. And before I left, I had him run through the one that seemed to mean the most to him, Polly, Nancy, and Muncimeg [microcard ed., No. 8; see also Chapter 6]. His visualization of the story was as clear as a bell and his telling was delightfully naive. He believed the story himself and cackled out in the tense passages, some of which he savored on his tongue with a second telling. I noticed the sparseness of words in the telling and the complete lack of elaboration. The gestures, the wide range of voice inflection, the dramatic pauses —these filled that lack. On paper the story seemed eroded and bare, and I had Jim tell it in his own way for print.

So much for the old man Tom, one of the best and most noted banjo men of eastern Kentucky.

Another member of the Couch family I met by an indirect route. Early in Jim's recording sessions he related the One-Eyed Giant [microcard ed., No. 7; see also Chapter 6], the old adventure of Ulysses and Sinbad the Sailor. This was the first American recording of this old epic fragment that I knew of, and I was anxious to trace it back as far as possible. Jim was willing to go with me into the Leatherwood country, across the Pine Mountain and to Clover Fork, to find old Basil Holbrook, who had told him the story.

Almost four years passed before we set out over the mountains on this quest. Jim pointed out the old big log house in a bend of the Clover Fork. We stopped and went toward the rustic houseseat, with its rived board roof, puncheoned floor, and beamed and raftered interior. There was an old rock well with its high wellsweep behind a peachtree grove in the garden. We found old Basil at home, retired from strenuous day labor. He was ailing this morning, but he was in a good mood to talk over old times. He was a rather large, stoutish man of perhaps seventy years, dressed in brown pants and chambray shirt open at the neck. In his life he had worked at everything—sawmilling, farming, moonshining (best maker in the country, Jim always said), and lastly, running a whisky store up the creek. No, he

hadn't told any stories in a long time; he had been too busy
until his family was raised and gone. But he remembered
clearly the very man who had told him the One-Eyed Giant.

"Now I heared that story," he said, "and a lot of others from
old John Couch, your great-uncle [i.e., great-uncle's son], Jim.
He was the very man told me that old story."

"Now is that a fact?" Jim asked, his mouth open.

And I said, "Well, Jim, looks as if this throws the old story
right back into the family tree. You men trace his descendants,
and we'll see if we can find out more about it and other stories."

"Why, that'll be easy," Basil said. "Jim, you orght to know
most of 'em well. They allas said that the first Couch to come
was old Lihew, and later two or three brothers. The brothers
settled down in here, but old Lihew [Anse's eldest son] moved
on down the river to the three forks of the Kentucky, around
Beattyville. And then he moved on to Owsley County. One
of his boys was John, and he used to come back in here, moved
here a time or two and lived off and on for years. That's when
I heared them stories from him. When he died, some of his
chillern lived down there and Virginia. You know most of 'em,
don't you, Jim?"

"Yeaw, I knowed ever' one of 'em well."

"Well, you had a grandpa John and this great-uncle John.
He's dead and didn't leave many chillern in here, but they's one.
That's Joe C—Little Joe they called him. The last time I heared
of him he was over yander at Appalachia, Virginia."

"Yeaw, I know he's over there," Jim said. "He lives over
there, and I've got a great-uncle Tom still over there sommers."

"Jim," I said, "looks like we had better be on our way to
Appalachia to trace this story and to see if Joe knows any others
that didn't come down to you."

The small town in the gorge of old Big Stone Mountain was
quiet when we drove into it at ten o'clock at night. All the
information we had was a name—Joe Couch. Up on a lost trail
above the town we shouted at the house of an old man, a relative
of the Couches. The family tree was traced again and other

friendly visiting before we got a new set of directions, this time to the old freight depot. With all of our equipment we had neglected to bring along a simple flashlight, and now we faced a long row of houses. A voice directed us farther on. We backed away to the outside of a fence and stumbled on to another opening—shouting again, mentioning names. We were in a back path, calling into kitchens. A noise from a dark porch, and a man approached to within five feet of us huddled in a backyard. He flourished a big pistol and demanded who we were, what we wanted. I hurriedly mentioned the name of Couch—we were visitors, relatives. The figure wavered and looked at us before walking to the next kitchen door and pushing it open. "Hey, dad," he said, "some men out here want to see you. All right, I reckon."

We were directed through the kitchen to the living room, and at last we had a good look at Joe and his wife and the only son at home. The two men talked about kinship and adventures. Joe was the excitable, talkative type. He was a small man, rather dark complexioned, lame in both legs. Before very long he had told about putting most of his life into mining, until the fatal day came for him. He was caught under a slab of slate fourteen feet square and many inches thick. The men who could get to him worked for four hours breaking the rock up with sledge hammers to rescue him. His legs were broken, his pelvis crushed, most ribs smashed like crushing a basket— all consigning him to the hospital for years.

"Can't walk to do no good now," he said, throwing his leg out of place at the knee and at the hip. "I was as good as dead and ever'body thought I was out of this world, and I don't know how I lived, but I made it.

"Yeaw, I used to know all them stories, but I've forgot 'em, man. Buddy, I used to tell stories all the time, but people don't tell stories like they used to. I've not been in a storytelling crowd in years." But it did develop before we went to bed that he knew most of the old Indian, pioneering, and Civil War legends that Jim and Dave had related. He knew a version of

the old One-Eyed Giant somewhat different from those of Jim
and Dave. He called it Johnny Sore-Nabel [microcard ed., No.
61], a nickname given by the giant to the hero because he had
skinned his belly. His twelve-year-old son helped to recall an
Old World tale that the other tellers had forgotten. Joe called
it The White Deer [microcard ed., No. 57]. Jim acknowledged
having heard it but said that he might never have thought of it.

The next morning the family went to their job in town—
cleaning the local bus station. Joe was anxious to show us his
garden that he had rented down in the valley, where we went
and found that he had undertaken a large garden project. We
helped him gather young corn and beans and tomatoes to bring
back. At last we had a long storytelling session, in which Joe
was able to contribute some fine old fairytales and many local
legends and shorter anecdotes.

By the time the stories were told, Joe's wife had dinner
ready. We all sat down to a delicious meal of steaming vegetables and hot coffee. Jim and I had been out on the road for
four days, and anxious to get back over Big Black Mountain,
we loaded our equipment and said goodbye.

The account of the Couch family would be incomplete if I
did not mention all the members and reveal some negative
results. There was Tom's oldest son Lewis, who had stayed in
the rural sections of Harlan and Perry counties all of his life,
but at no time would Jim or Mandy name him as a good storyteller. I saw him and talked with him, and although he seemed
to have remembered some of the older fairytales and perhaps
told them on occasion, he had laid them aside. His children had
long ago grown up and left home, but he had two grandchildren
living beside him on Laurel Fork, and they came to Pine
Mountain School. I had one, a boy of thirteen, in the seventh
grade. He thought a great deal of his grandfather and often
said that he could tell tales and liked to talk. But the only items
that the boy could give me were local legends, hunting stories,
and a few puzzles and riddles. Apparently the oldest son of
Tom did not make the effort necessary to be a folklore per-

former, and Jim had said as much to me when we discussed the family performers.

There was the daughter Sally, living two miles below Putney with her houseful of children. I was interested in her earlier banjo picking and performing days. She was entirely negative on the subject. She once liked to sing ballads but had not kept it up. "I don't know any no more," she would say; "Jim and Dave have kept on telling them tales and singing the ballads."

As for the two youngest sons Alex and Harrison, I had two different reactions. Alex was the shy man of the group and apparently had never let a story or song pass his lips. He was a quiet, serious, hard worker. The youngest child of the family, Harrison, was evidently too young to have heard his mother tell tales in the home. The family, as we know, scattered when the mother died, and Harrison had never learned the family traditions. He had come to be looked on by the other members as the scholar of the group, and perhaps he had gone to high school. Through work in the church he had become a song leader and finally had made his way to song teacher and had conducted simple singing schools in the churches of the valley. Jim referred me to him for hymns and moral songs. But during collecting times I always found Harrison too busy to perform, and if he had, I am not sure that he would have known many items of traditional lore. He was busy at his store by the roadside and at times taking jobs in the community and at times mining coal with his brothers. When I approached him on one occasion, he seemed to feel that Jim and Dave should have the credit for putting together the family lore and (he intimated) they should be the sharers in its success and in its monetary rewards.

These reminiscences of Jim, Dave, and other members of the family touch on many aspects of mountain life that perhaps can be summarized. From their accounts of earning a living and of enjoying their leisure we can comment upon the society of which they were a part, with its unique family, social, and environmental conditions.

The family in a rural community is in fact as well as in theory the unit of culture. The unit, from two to a dozen or more, lives under one roof and provides everything it needs, and what it cannot provide, it does without. The bigger the family the better. Some family heads go forth to multiply and replenish the earth under biblical command. They have as many children as nature provides, and they welcome each and every one. Mrs. Mary Breckinridge, director of the Frontier Nursing Service in Leslie County, says that the easiest births and the healthiest and most wanted babies in the world are in eastern Kentucky. As the family grows, each member has a place and a status, and each one has work to do in keeping the unit self-sustaining.

The most important member and the undisputed head of the family unit is the father. Almost without exception he controls, directs, and leads the family like the Patriarchs of old. When called upon or referred to in any way, he is usually called "the man of the house." While he is talking business with another man, the wife and children stay in the background, the mother usually collecting the children into a back room and going on with her work. If the business concerns the father only, he will take his time and consider the whole unit, but in the end he will make his own decision. If the business involves other members, the mother, for instance, the father will state the gist of it to her and leave her alone to think it over. She will reach a decision, mention it to the father conditionally, and he will accept, modify, or reject it as he sees fit. This dominant status of the father is in no way peculiar to Kentucky mountain people. It is somewhat typical of family units over the world and especially those forebears of ours of Scotch-Irish background. Their hardships on poor acres and their dark and fatalistic outlook on life under Calvinism have made them stern and undemonstrative.

The position of the wife and mother in a mountain home has always been a trying and a difficult one. Her endless chores around a household without conveniences wear her down and bring her to an early grave. She is expected to take care of the clothing from making to mending and of the food from tending the pigs and garden to preserving the meat and vegetables and serving them on the table three times a day. Meanwhile, she is giving her life day by day to her growing children and her strength to the bearing of more. It is not uncommon to find a man of the mountains who has worn out two or three wives in this round of endless sacrifice.

The undemonstrative nature of mountain people is completely dissolved with children. As was said above, each child is wanted, and when one comes, he is treated with an indulgence that surpasses understanding. The grandparents come and dandle him and "make over" him, and perhaps before he is standing alone, one or the other has claimed him and even given him a nickname that he will bear through life. The parents fondle him with unfeigned love, as do the older children. The baby is breastfed until the next one is on the way, and he is allowed to sleep with the mother or with both parents. When old enough, he is allowed to crawl throughout the house, next to toddle indoors and out, and finally, when he can run about, he is allowed to follow the older people to the fields and about the neighborhood.

But at six or seven he begins to make himself useful at running errands and performing other duties suitable to his age. If he is the oldest child in the home, he will soon take on responsibilities that make him seem older than he actually is. By young manhood he has taken on a kind of fierce individuality among the other members of the group. Each succeeding child struggles for and is given a great deal of personal liberty and respect. Certain traits, abilities, and talents appear in each, and he is free to shine in them. One son can handle the horses better than another; one can manage the mowing machine better; one can better grind the ax and sharpen the saws; one shows up early in school and is called the learner. But also one may be a little hard to manage, be balky and "contrary," and become the male Cinderella with his feet in the ashes most of the time. Most large families have one who is known to all as the "black sheep."

There is a close parallel between such a mountain household and the Couch family. The parallel need not be drawn at all points. Tom Couch had an average-to-large family, as sizes go in the mountains. He was the leader, and the mother was the counselor of the unit. The children developed along natural lines and came out distinct personalities in adult life.

But this family appears to me to be a little unusual in some respects. They seem to have got along better than the average, their life having a little more quality and distinction than the typical. The father was not so stern and forbidding as some; on the contrary, he put more life and zest into living and had ways that drew his children out. He had a skill that was looked up to in the home and community—playing the banjo and singing. And all of his children tried to emulate him. The indelible little picture given by Jim may illustrate his way with them. Jim began to pick up the banjo when he was seven or eight, too short to reach both head and neck of the instrument. His father fingered the strings while he beat out the tune and the rhythm. A similar illustration may suffice for the mother's ways. While waiting for the father to come home at night, she beguiled the children and held them from the table with animal and giant stories.

One other factor making the Couch family different appears to me to be that of good native intelligence. Of book learning they had very little, for the simple reason that it was not to be had. But the fact that the members of the family were able to adapt themselves to one another and to the larger community, to draw into the family unit most of the skills of farming, mining, lumbering, and to retain most of the inherited lore, to add to it, and to pass it on indicates above-average mental powers. A few instances of clearheaded powers of retention may be given. Old Tom actually sang from beginning to end every song we asked him to recall, though he was ninety-two at the

time and had not played the banjo in twenty years. Dave
recalled and told a long story that he had not heard or even
thought of in thirty-five years. When Jim was ten years old, he
went with his father to a still in the woods, and on that night
the great Halley's comet appeared. He remembered not only
the event but also the look in the men's eyes, the words they
said, and how the mash barrel he was grasping seemed to
tremble as he shivered. Sensitive and unclouded minds such
as these are able to respond to the stimuli about them.

Another condition that must be taken into account for
understanding a Kentucky mountain family such as that of the
Couches is the environment. The earliest Couches came into
Kentucky when it was still the Promised Land, when there was
still an abundance of free land or cheap land to be taken up
by simple patent. They built their cabins in isolated creeks
and branches, and lived by farming and hunting. One of their
largest problems was to clear the land and to dig in some corn
and beans by hand. Neighbors were few and far between, and
their isolation threw them upon their own resources. The first
generations fought the bears and panthers that later generations
told about in chimney corners. All communication, all knowledge, and all recreation were handed down orally. Up until
the First World War there were no distractions from passing
cars, from phonographs, from radios; at the present time there
is little interference from telephones, newspapers, television.

The people lived in the quiet, peaceful valley. They were in
tune with the changing days and the changing seasons. Each
hour of the day had its significance, from the break of dawn
and the crowing of the cock to late evening with the flicker of
fireflies and the croaking of frogs. Indoors before early retire-
ment all was still except for the crackling of the fire and the
ticking of the clock. Work that went on then was handicrafts
—smoothing an ax handle, fashioning a rag doll, carding the
wool, spinning, knitting. Any recreation was performed by the
family members from the store of lore and folkways handed

down from the old folks—hul-gul with grains of parched corn, tales, legends, fox and geese with homemade board, ballads that told some tragic story.

Nights and days like these were lived by the Couches. And whatever lore they retained as they scattered to the settlements and to the more populated areas was learned by repeating it and reliving it in their isolated cabins on Sang Branch, on the Clover Fork of Big Leatherwood, and in other quiet valleys.

Though families such as the Couches lived in isolation, especially in the earlier generations, they did get together in many ways. They suffered isolation because they had to, and they broke that isolation as often and as long as possible. The three greatest socializing forces were religion, labor, and recreation, the people sometimes combining two, or even all three of them.

Old Tom Couch was not a churchgoer and apparently never joined any church. When he was growing up, there was perhaps no church for him to join, because organized religion came late to the long-isolated valleys of eastern Kentucky. At first the people had only visiting preachers who held meetings at the forks of the creek once a month when weather permitted and crops were "laid by." Through the long winters they came not at all, and this gave rise to long protracted meetings in the spring, annual associations, and what came to be called funeral-izings. Simply stated, this last custom was the preaching of the funerals in good weather of all those who had died during the long winters when ministers could not be called. (It also meant a series of weddings—for those who had been married by a civil officer and wanted also a religious wedding, for those who had been waiting for a minister to show up, and for those who had not waited.)

As time went on, more preachers appeared, church was held twice a month, laymen felt the call, and churches were built, especially in the lower, more thickly settled river valleys. But to this day many isolated valleys have no regular or lay preacher, and some do not have a churchhouse.

The fact that Tom Couch was not overly religious was apparently a favorable factor in the preservation of the lore of the family. He did not govern its members with too many *don'ts* and *thou shalt nots*. As Jim put it, "We just worked all day and played all night, about it." Although the mother went to church with the children and at times stayed all day, with dinner on the ground, she told the old stories to the family and welcomed a party at her house after a bean-stringing bee.

These bees were indeed an important socializing force among eastern Kentucky people. In early, laborious days they were true communal exchanges of labor. Six or eight families in a portion of a valley had about the same phases of work to do at about the same time. The able-bodied hands went to each other's homes and worked the crop, or raised a house or barn, or cleared a patch of land, or harvested the corn and wheat. The women took baskets of food and prepared it at the host's house for all to eat together. A game time by the younger set for part of the night was almost as necessary as the main task. When the beans were to be strung, the apples to be peeled, or the corn to be husked, the folk assembled to these lighter tasks as a pretext for a playparty the remainder of the night.

At these gatherings the Couches, some of them at least, had a chance to shine. Old Tom played the banjo for the sets and other musical games until he had raised a son to take his place. Dave early became the favorite son with the banjo, and the fact that he never learned to dance a set attests to his long and faithful service as musician. Jim apparently preferred to be down among the lasses, since he became adept at organizing games and calling squares and other folkdance sets.

Thus we see how one family inherited a store of oral traditions and through their own intelligence, industry, and desire for social acceptance and approval made the most of it. Old Tom gathered songs from all sources and fed them into the heritage. Mandy married and settled in another isolated valley. Soon she was telling the mother's stories to her own children, and when Jim came to live with her, she refreshed his memory with their haunting mystery. Jim in turn began to excel as a storyteller with the family store, to which he added the legends and yarns of many other men. Dave, continuing to play the banjo for dances long after he was married, kept the title as favorite banjo picker. He contributed most of the hundred folksongs to this collection, while Jim recorded most of the sixty stories.

CHAPTER 4

JIM AND DAVE, THEIR MOONSHINING

"HOLD IT a minute," Jim stopped me one Sunday morning when I was just ready to start the tape recorder. He reached into his inside coat pocket and pulled out a small bottle nearly full of clear, beady liquid. Taking a couple of gurgles, he smacked his lips and extended it to me. One little swallow went down me like a red-hot ball bearing and rolled around at the bottom of my stomach. Jim deliberately gave me time to decide if I had had enough before extending his hand for it, giving it another little dash on his tongue before replacing the bottle.

"Ready to go! Ahmmmmmmmm. Let me sorter study now about my long experiences with moonshining. I'll tell you the best un that ever happened when I was at a moonshine still —and the scariest un. My daddy was a-making whisky over there in a holler on the Sang Branch. He never had till then let me go with him to his still because I's just eight or nine year old. He come in home and got supper for the men at the still, and I bagged to go back with him. He took me along and I got to see my first run o' moonshine.

"The reason I can remember it so well—we got back there to that old still, and they had it farred up and was a-running whisky to beat the band. They set down and eat and got through and was having a big-eyed time, there under the timber. All was a-drinking and everything was a-going good. Then they all looked back toward the east and saw something a-coming through the evedence [elements]. When they saw it coming, somebody called it a great comic [comet], and they begin to say, 'Lord how [have] mercy, the end of time is a-coming.' They begin to draw the far out from under that old still —like that would save 'em, you know. We set there and couldn't move while it was passing on over. I was standing there holding on to a mash barrel and my knees just a-giving it that. But finally it went down kindly in the southwest. Oh, it was just like a big light, or the sun shining for a while. It looked to me about like a ball the size of a half bushel, and it had a tail to it that looked to be about twenty feet long.

"It disappeared in several minutes, down under the hill, and then we heared a big explosion, and that barrel shook where I was a-hold of it. They claimed it busted. After a while they all eased up and decided the end was not a-going to come, leastways not that night, and commenced to fanning the far back up. They went on and made a purty good run the rest of the night."

"Do you know now what that was?" I interjected. "That was Halley's comet, that visited the earth in 1910—it is due to come back in seventy-five years—"

"I don't care when she comes back," Jim countered. "I'll remember that night till she comes again, I guess. When I heared ever'body a-moaning and carrying on, I was about to have heart failure.

"Well, I hope my dad make liquor a lot after that, but I didn't actually learn how from him. The man that learnt me to make whisky he was a professional moonshiner. He was give up to be the best in the mountain parts. That was old Hiram Holbrooks over on Leatherwood.

"Now the way you begin making whisky, you carry your old barrels to the place, in some holler where they are plenty of water. A still is a thing you can make. You take and get you a sheet of copper the size you want to make your still, large or small, and you take some brass brads and put that thing in the form of a barrel. Then you take plank and make a head for this still. After that you want a hole in this head, so you take a auger and handsaw and saw a round hole in the head for your cap, whatever cap you want. It's a kag about twelve inches, I guess.

"But start with your mash first in the copper still. Take and heat your water boiling, then you take meal. Pour your meal in the barrel, and then you pour in your water. You stir this meal up until you cook it good. You keep right on adding meal and water until you cook it right into a mush. Well, when you get it cooked to your notion, you take about a quart of flour to ever' barrel, and put it right down on top of your mash to hold your heat in. 'Ell, we let that set over to the next day, let it get good and cool.

"And then we take an old sausage mill to grind our malt corn. We'd sprout what was called malt corn. Take and put corn in a coffee sack in water until it sprouted good, until good long sprouts come on it. Then we'd take this mill and grind this malt corn up, about a kag to a barrel. And we'd go back and put this malt corn in that barrel. And then you take your hands like making dough, and you bust ever' lump in there. Stir just like making gravy, to get it all dissolved just like milk. And then you cover your barrel real good, and in about three days this meal will go to working. You've seen slop, now, be setting in a bucket in hot times, come up in big bubbles and bust. That's the way mash works. It'll work in about three or four days sometimes.

"Then it'll clear off, and all that meal will settle back in the bottom. And then we'll go ahead and get a forked stick, and we'll get into them barrels, and we'll stir all that up together. We'll take and build us a far and heat that until it turns into a simmer, beginning to get ready to boil. Then we take our cap, put a stick with a hole in it down in the cap, and put it in that hole in the still. And then we'll take clay mud and daub all the steam in there. The steam is coming out the hole in your cap. We have a piece of wood, oh, usually about two feet long, sourwood. Take it and bore me a hole in it. Start in at one end and bore as fer as I can, and then start at the other end and bore the hole out. We use that fer an arm.

We put that in that still cap, and we'll daub it in there. Well, we'll put a worm in it if we're making the old-fashioned way —we'll take our worm then and put in the other end of that arm, and we'll daub her in there good. And of course if we're making it with a crooked worm, we'll have a barrel to put that worm in; and if we're making with a straight worm, we'll have a trough made and a hole bored in each end of it, and the worm would run through it for our water to pour in on.

"That goes to boiling in the still, and the steam comes out into that worm and evaporates in the worm, and when it comes out to the end, we catch it and call it singlings. It's an alkiehol, but not high-powered alkiehol. It runs a stream about the size of a number-eight nail. Well, we'll run these singlings off, about eight or ten gallons, sometimes twelve.

"I'll have this still full of singlings and go back and pour 'em in a barrel. I'll go right back and repeat it over and over till I'll get me a barrel of this what I call singlings. Well, now I'll take my old still apart and wash and scrub it. Have to wash ever'thing thoroughly clean—worm, arm, still, cap, and ever' thing. Take you about three hours or three hours and a half to get it cleaned up ready for your second run.

"Then I'll put these singlings back in the still. Get 'em on the far now and get 'em to boiling, just up in the center, like you was a-making sorghum, you know, when they go to foaming up in the pan. I'll cap 'em up like I did in the first place. Well, I'll pull my far down to a very small far—you wouldn't want to overheat it. Just heat it enough to get it started to boil good enough, and then just keep a small steady far under it. Keep about one temperature all the time. About an hour after you capped your still up again, your first shots of alkiehol begin to run. Two hundred proof. You'd catch that in a jar or jug, whatever you wanted to catch 'em in. Set it around. I always mark mine—number one, two, three, four, like that. Catch it in a gallon fruit jar or gallon jug. Sometimes I'd catch it in a gallon jug.

"When I'd get this run off down to where it gets so weak it

wouldn't bead—you see, it is too strong to bead when it first comes out of a run like we're speaking of; sometimes you can catch ten or twelve gallons too strong to bead—well, then you catch you so much and this is good beading whisky, about ninety to a hundred to hundred and ten proof. Then it runs down until it won't bead a-tall. And we call that backings. Then I'll catch a half a bushel of these backings, and then I'll cut it all off and get ready to make my whisky.

"Take my first shots, my middle batch, and my weak batch, and I'll get me two old washtubs. I'll put me so much of one kind in there and so much of another. Take me a stick and keep it stirred up good. I'll keep a-tasting, you know, clear down in the bottom, and shaking it. I'd put some in a bottle and give it three shakes and turn it back upright. Get the bead of the whisky till it would be the size of a squirrel's eye—that's the way I allas judged it. I'd have a hundred and ten proof whisky. And I'd keep on that way till I got my whole batch o' whisky just the way I wanted it. Jar it up and go to selling it then.

"That's the way I started making whisky and the way I run it when I didn't have more than five barrels of mash to run off. But if I was making up to thirty barrel and making in a big fashion, I'd have to have two stills, a hundred gallon and a thirty. I'd take this hundred-gallon still, and of course I sugared that time—put sugar in it and that made a lot more and stronger singlings. I'd run this big still full into singlings and put that in the little still, and I'd have both going at oncet. Build me a furnace on the left and a furnace on the right, and each one meeting the other. I have at times used the same trough for both worms. Take the singlings from the big still and put in the little, and keep 'em both going that a-way.

"I saw some big stills in Louisville a few months ago, but I couldn't tell what they was trying to do. Went down there to see my two sons. Had a purty good time and found my boys working ever' day and one of 'em took me out to see a big 'stillery. They make plenty o' whisky down there, but when

we went through, we didn't see a thing in there but old big
barrels and vats. Of course they color their whisky—bonded, it
is called—and cut down on the proof. I never did see a man in
here but wouldn't druther have moonshine—if it is made right
—than bonded colored stuff. Now buddy, I guess I've made in
my lifetime about as much as they had mashed up in there and
in stock.

"Well, the stuff I've just told you to make was straight corn
whisky. For it you don't put a thing in it but just your meal
and malt corn and the flour on top to keep in the heat. There
is as much difference between corn and sugar whisky as they
are in between sweet milk and sour milk. Straight corn whisky
has got a sweet mellow mild taste. You can drink all of it you
want and hardly ever get a headache. You can drink it and get
too much on your stomach, and you can belch and spit it up.
You take sugar whisky, and if you get too much of that, it comes
back the hard way; you think your stomach and all is coming
up with it. Straight corn sells for about four times what you
get for sugar liquor. Sometimes if you have good luck, you get
two gallons and a quart of straight out of one barrel.

"Now we are going to put up some sugar mash. Get you a
sixty-gallon barrel and make her full up of meal and water like
we done before, but instid of putting malt in it, you put in
fifty pounds of sugar and stir that up good and let it set. And
when you run it, you can get about eight gallons of sugartop
whisky. Now I never did run sugartop in the old-fashioned way.
Takes too much time handling all them singlings. For the other
way a-making, then, we put in what is called a thumping kag.
The way a thumping kag works, you hook your old still up just
like I explained, but you would have your thumping kag at the
end of the arm where the worm connected in the old-fashioned
still. You have you a ten-gallon barrel a-setting there and drill
you a hole in it, and let your arm reach down in it about six or
eight inches. On the other side of this kag we drill another
hole down in the top and make us another chuck [wooden pipe].
This reaches to the bottom of the kag. We put an arm on this

chuck a foot or two long and connect our worm to it. Use a coil worm and put it in your flake barrel. This gives us a thumping kag between our worm and our still.

"The steam runs from that still into this thumping kag, and we catch about four gallons of singlings and take them and pour 'em in the thumping kag. And then when the steam goes into that thumping kag, it comes out of there good whisky from then on as long as you run, you see. You don't have to take it out and clean up ever'thing the way we did the other way. If you've got fifty barrels of mash, you can run all of 'em ever'time you put that still up.

"I learned most about a still by going and helping my dad. But over there on Leatherwood I got to helping old Hiram Holbrooks, and he was a regular old moonshiner, the best in there. I was purty well experienced before I went off to the army. After I come back, I made with my brother a right smart. An old man of Evarts town was a regular old drinker. My brothers-in-law went over there on a timber job and found out I's making, and they would get some on weekends and take it back. That old man got hold of some of that and wanted more. They had taken some in an old bottle, I called it a turtle shell, the only one I had seen in my life like it.

"Well, I was setting up there on the railroad track. Looked down the road and saw five men a-coming up, and I didn't know neither one of them from sight. I said to myself, 'They're damn revenues right now.' They come up and set down beside me and asked me about some whisky. I told them hell about whisky, I didn't know anything about whisky.

"The signal was that bottle I had let the boys have. They told me who they was, but I didn't believe them. Showed me that bottle. 'Well,' I said, 'you must be telling the truth.' I said, 'If you hain't, you must be sons o' bitches.'

"They said they wasn't no law. I showed 'em I had my forty-five on. I said, 'I've got whisky—a-plenty.'

"I went off down the road with 'em and sold twenty-five

gallons that night. It was sugar, and I got five dollars a gallon for it.

"One time my brother was making and had a feller helping him. They heared the revenues was hunting for 'em in that country, and they was scared to go to their still. They told me if I would run that run off for 'em, they'd pay me five dollars a day and ten dollars a night. They had sebemteen barrels mashed up. I didn't have no fambly, single, and about fourteen or fifteen years old. I took 'em up.

"I went to running that whisky, and I had sixty-eight gallons run off. Stored it back in the hill. I was a-setting there, and the old thumping kag was just a-clucking. Seemed to me you could hear it thirty yards off. Making right in the edge of an old field, where a little holler came, and they had dug out in the bank and you could look over there from the field and couldn't see a thing. I was a-setting there one night running, just about done anyhow. I had a 30-30 marlin rifle gun setting beside me. I knowed I's a-bucking the law and weren't afraid of nothing.

"They'd hunted in that branch about all day. I peeped out in that old field, and there was one of them revenues, so clost to me I could see him bat his eyes. He was looking right up the holler. And he never did spy me. I scooted around the hill and got hold of my rifle. I thinks to myself, 'Old feller, if you come on up here, I'll drop you right here.'

"I had that right in my mind. The old feller turned off and went back down the hill about thirty yards. They was six or eight of them, and they come that nigh a-getting my whisky and mash. I'd got away. I'd went right over a little bank and could have been gone if they had ventured up. They never did see no smoke. You can't see any steam from a still but only of the morning or late about dusky dark. You can't smell it or the still coming up, but you can coming down. They's in below it.

"I'll now tell you about how I got along back in Hoover's

administration. You know, times got awful hard. We's logging
at the time, but they had to shet down. We couldn't sell lumber,
and ever'body just quit and nobody had no money saved.

"Some of the boys went to Evarts and took a timber job,
just to make enough to feed their stock. They wanted me to
go with 'em, but I had a purty good sized crop out that year.
I couldn't leave it, and I took a notion to crop and make whisky.
It was selling for four dollars a gallon—when you could sell it.

"Now I went to making it. Put me up some mash and went
and borrowed me an old still and worm. Mashed up one barrel
and run that off. I think I made a gallon and three quarts of
whisky. Well, I turned right around and mashed that barrel
up and set my whisky back. I sawed me two old holler linn
gums and reamed 'em out for barrels to mash in. The next run
I made twenty-eight gallons. I kept on making it and storing
it away, couldn't sell it much. I'd buy back materials and make
whisky, 'cause I knowed the times weren't going to stay that
bad allas. I made the most I ever had on hand at one time;
I'd salted away 168 gallons.

"I found out that the revenue men was looking for me. A
boy down at Barbourville—I had soldiered with him—turned me
in. They come up there on Greasy Creek and talked with a
feller. He told 'em, 'He's making somewhere on that branch,
but I don't know exactly where.' They looked all day and up
into the night. I knowed it, but made right on.

"I was standing there by the old still, putting jars under the
worm and taking the full ones out. I'd drunk all the beer
[mash] I wanted, nearly made me high. I's standing there, and
I heard a noise out through the tree tops where old timber had
been cut. I clomb up on a little hickory pole that I had cut
right at the mouth of the dreen [drain], just sawed him down
and never cut him plumb off. Left it on the stump with green
leaves on it so they couldn't see in there. The rest of my still
was surrounded with earth. I was ready with my pistol, standing
there ready, and that noise kept on coming right at me and my
still and all that whisky stored away there. It was getting about

dusky dark, and I couldn't see good. I was peeping through the underbrush, and all at once an old white-faced hog peeked his head through there. Tell you the truth, I never come more nigh fainting in all my life. I never thought about my pistol when that damn hog stuck his head through that bresh.

"I'll tell you one more, and it will give you an idea how we carried on in our whisky making. Back when I was young, we made whisky along a little 'cause it was about the only way we had to collect up any money to keep ourselves in clothing and ever'thing. We made our eats on the farm, and we'd get out and 'still up some whisky for tax money, you know, and so forth. We'd play jokes on one another. Maybe they'd be one still in this holler and maybe a half a mile away would be another in that holler. It'd just be a chance and time that a revenue would come around to hunt up our still. We had signals worked out to warn us. If the people at the mouth of a creek spied any revenues coming into the valley, they was supposed to ring the old dinner bell or shoot three shots. If we heared ary one, we knowed to sail out of there across the point.

"Two fellers was making in a holler when I was staying with my sister Mandy, and I took a notion to make me a run or two with 'em and mashed me up an old barrel or two. One of these men didn't care for nothing, but the other was awful scary. He was all the time looking for the law. One night they sunt me to get the supper. We'd been running for about three days. And I went and got the supper and took a notion I'd play a prank on them two fellers. I got one of the womenfolk to promise to toll the bell after so long. Most of the time the women wouldn't want to shoot a gun. Instid of me going back up the holler, I went out across the point and up in behind them. It was getting about dusky dark. The timber was green, but they'd been a storm blowed out an old limb and the leaves had dried on it. It was nearly right straight off to where they's at. That old bell begun to toll out, and I laid holt of that old bresh and started running down the hill. It went like a army a-coming.

"That scary feller jumped up and left there, and he never come back there that night. The other one he run out to the mouth of the holler, it scared him so bad. I went down there and laughed all I wanted to and stayed with the old still. Along late in the night he took a notion he'd come back. I looked down the holler—the moon was kindly shining—and I'd see him peep up out of the branch next to the timber line. He'd come out and peep and then slink back a piece. When they found out it was me, you talk about a ragging, boy, I got it.

"Well, sir, I never was caught at a still, what time I was making, and I've made as much as any man in these hills. The law wa'n't bad to hunt us down, even if they knowed we was making. They knowed they couldn't enforce the law, and if a man kept it quiet, they never bothered him. I've even had the local forces to tell me to stay outten the hills—when they heared some revenue was coming to get up a raid. Course they knowed I's a-making, but they knowed that I's a law-abiding man in ever'thing else, had a fambly and had to eat and pay taxes. They never did ketch me."

"Now I've made a good lot of moonshine in my time," Dave said in his turn. "I begun when we lived back in Perry County. My dad was making then, but I learnt from old Hiram Holbrooks. He was the moonshiningest man that ever made in Perry County and was said to make the best whisky that was made anywhere in the state. I started with him. He liked me and wanted me to learn how. He give me three bushel of corn to start on. I took it to the mill and had it ground into meal. Then he give me a half a bushel of corn to sprout and make into malt corn to use in my mash. And I mashed with him, put up a run with him on the Clover Fork of Leatherwood Creek, the first moonshining I ever done. He was the one that made it. I just stayed with him, packed water and stuff for him, and done whatever I could and he wanted me to. He was the man that made that batch, 'cause I was only just about fifteen, going on sixteen then. My part was about forty gallons that time. I stayed away from my mother and tried to keep it hid from her.

She found out I's a-making, and she bagged and convinced me to sell what I had made and go out to the Pine Mountain School and work and not make moonshine. Well, I wanted to mind my mother, something I allas tried to do. Well, after she died, then, I didn't have nobody to 'suade me not to make moonshine, and I went back, through bad company and 'suaded by violators, to making whisky again on Gabe's Branch.

"I made there for fourteen months in one place, and hoping old man Holbrooks learnt me how to make. Well, we had three stills up and outfits in the same holler. It was in a cleared field except a brush thicket by a watercourse. We made for fourteen months right in the middle of that brush thicket. I didn't do anything but make; the other party he carried it off and done the selling. He allowed his men to come to where I's making so I could load 'em up there, somebody we knowed. I stayed there and made day and night. In the daytime we would have a watch to look out for us for revenues. The watch would get out in a place where he could see fairly everywheres and not let 'em get on us too close. We had a sign for 'em, and we'd know what it meant. If they farred one shot, it would mean that bootlaggers was coming after whisky, and not be afeared. Well, two shots meant that some people was going by the road and no harm in them. But with three shots it was the revenues, and watch out. And when they would far three shots, we grabbed everything setting loose and lit out of there. Any whisky setting around we would get away to the bushes, and sometimes we could get everything out. If it was a false alarm, or if they missed us and went to some other place, we would stay low for a day or two and keep an eye on the revenues and see where they went to and when they got out of there before we went back to making.

"I made there for fourteen months and never got raided till a certain party who was making with us got mad. He told me he was going to have me cut up. He was going to bring 'em and show 'em the place. Well, I had my watchman out and was trying to run off what I had mashed up. I would run a barrel

off and have the barrel carried off and saved. I had it all run
off but two barrel and had forty-some gallons of whisky carried
off and hid. I got the alarm that the revenue was in. I had to
leave there and also leave sebem gallons of whisky and my still
there. I didn't have much there 'cause I's not going to mash
back when I's going to get raided and cut up. I got in the clear,
and they come and cut up what was left and taken the moonshine. I guess they thought they got all I had, but they didn't.
You see, we had three stills that we run at the same time to get
along faster, and we had two of them out of the way and nearly
all of the other'n. They got two of my barrels and them full of
beer—I was going to run them that night. Well, after they cut
that un up and left, I went back the next day and went to
putting me up a furnace at another place, about three hundred
yards above where I had been making, but in another holler. I
made there for about five months without any trouble. But
some parties from over on Bailey's Creek, bootlaggers, got so
bad with it they got indicted all over the place. Then they lit
into us. Old man Wright Winn indicted me on five counts
—operating moonshine still, selling moonshine whisky, trans-
porting moonshine whisky. The law was hard on moonshining
then, and if they handled ye, they could give ye two year. Well,
I studied it would be better for me to leave there then and not
be 'rested on them cases than to have trial. So I left.

"I went to the C. & O. Railroad and got me a job about sebem
mile from Hazard. I worked on the railroad and bootlagged
all the time, but I didn't make any. Bootlaggers would come in
there with a load, and I'd buy 'em out and peddle it out of a
night while I worked of a day, or peddle of a day while I worked
of a night. Made a profit on it. Bootlagged all the time I was
there for twenty-sebem months and never got turned up for it.
I come back acrost the Pine Mountain to my brother's and
stayed there and bootlagged awhile. The law didn't run out
for five year, and I still had them indictments again' me, you
see. I dodged for nearly five year, and the old feller that indicted me died and passed on. I went to Bailey's Creek then

and got me a job loading coal. But I still sold whisky, sold it
right on. Loaded coal of a day, come back acrost Pine Mountain
where I moonshined and bootlagged all the time, buy me a
load of whisky and pack it over there and bootlag it out. I
carried it on my back, four gallon in a sack, across Pine Mountain, then across Gabe's Mountain, and on to Bailey's Creek.
Most of the time I'd carry it across three mountains—Cutshin
Mountain, Gabe's Mountain, and Pine Mountain. Even sometimes I'd go on through Bailey's Creek and carry it across Black
Mountain.

"I remember they's a cornival [carnival] in at Evarts in below
Bailey's Creek one time. I was working at the Bailey's Creek
mine and found out about that cornival to come in there, and
I made three trips across them mountains, carried twelve gallon
of whisky over there, and hid it. And the night of the cornival
I sold all them twelve gallon of moonshine. Sold it for forty
dollars a gallon.

"But my money never did do me no good I got out of whisky.
It come easy and it went easy. And I believe today the reason
I never got nothing out of whisky making was 'cause my mother
was all the time again' it and she told me never to do it and
she bagged me not to. But I went ahead, after she left here,
going again' her will. And I think that is the reason the money
I got out of whisky never done me no good.

"Well sir, I guess I made over 10,000 gallon of whisky all told.
I wouldn't have no ideas, but I know I've made more than that.
And I sold five times more than I made. But I don't make none
now; I hain't drunk a drap of whisky in sixteen year, won't fool
with it no way, makes me mad ever' time I see it, can't stand to
smell it, can't stand to be where it's at—I don't want a thing to
do with it. After I got up in my late years I realized what I'd
done back in the first part of my days, spent all the good part
of my life violating the law and doing things that my mother
didn't want me to. I see where I missed it. And my father he
is ninety-sebem years old and living today, and I have had
several nar' ex-capes from the law. After I was first married and

living on Bailey's Creek, I had a lot of whisky in the house. Had
sebem gallon in a box and had a few layers of empty fruit jars
on top. They were searching for goods that had been stole
from camp. They went all over my house and finally come to
that box and commenced setting them empties out of there. Got
down through some of the last layer and one of 'em said, 'Well,
I don't reckon he's got anything in there. They look like they
are all empty.' I come that nigh getting catched and taken off
then.

"I went to work—"

Dave's wife had heard what he was recording and came
hurriedly to the door at this moment. Just as he finished the
last paragraph, she spoke up, "I'd be ashamed to tell it. I would,
I'd be ashamed to tell it, to let my younguns hear me tell sech
stuff as that."

The session was over.

Jim's and Dave's stories of making whisky give us a rather
vivid picture of the process, as well as some of the danger and
trouble involved. To look at their record alone we may be
prompted to condemn them for contributing to the problems
of the region and for disregarding the law. But perhaps their
case can be lightened, or at least partially explained, by sketch-
ing in the background of whisky making among the people of
Kentucky.

Whisky making has always been a handicraft among the
English, Scottish, and Irish from the Middle Ages, as names
like Brewer and Bracer still testify. The process has been
handed down from household to household as other crafts and
skills have been. Settlers of the land west of the Appalachians,
largely peoples from the British Isles, brought their habits and
folkways with them. As soon as the people found a valley to
their liking in eastern Kentucky, they continued their self-suf-
ficient way of life, making by hand all that they possessed.
When they had more of any commodity than they needed for
themselves, they sold it for money to pay taxes and to buy
"brought on" necessities. The marketing of timber alone, with

the struggles and hardships involved, makes a sagalike story. The men had to cut the timber and run it to the bottom of the hill, where they built a splashdam across the creek to make a flood when needed to carry the logs out to the larger streams. Here the logs were made up into rafts with rudder and tiller and were left until the spring rises and floods. Men then guided the crafts down winding, flooded rivers to the lowland markets.

Enterprising men who had a little money ahead bought up the people's cattle and drove them in large herds over winding upland trails to the railheads in the Bluegrass, a distance of sometimes 150 miles. They drove herds of sheep and hogs and flocks of turkeys and geese out of the mountains in the same way. They were able in this way to make their produce walk to market.

This could not be done with grain, fruit, and vegetables. The latter two commodities were preserved in profusion for home use and for barter among the neighbors. As for the grain, it helped to fatten the stock, and what was left over was turned into whisky, put up in barrels, and hauled out. In the Bluegrass it found its way to the keelboat wharves and went down the rivers to New Orleans. By the time of the Civil War whisky had become one of the chief sources of money income, principally because it was a steady source of income, whereas the timber, the herds, and the flocks were seasonal products. But dating from the time of that war, whisky has been taxed, at times so heavily as to be punitive. The tax most of the time has equaled or exceeded the manufacturing cost of the product. And from that day to this, more and more whisky has gone underground: it has been made by moonlight in hidden places, put up in smaller containers, transported in the bootlegs and saddlepockets of "blockaders," and sold outside the usual channels of trade.

The control of unlicensed whisky makers up until 1918 was in the hands of state officials. The officers of the smallest unit of government, the county, were the county judge, the high sheriff, and his district subordinates, the constables. These men, especially the sheriff and his deputies, were acquainted with every family in the county—they had to assess property, issue various licenses, collect taxes, and keep records of the people from births to deaths. When we realize that the county officials were often related to many families in the county, had to rely on the citizens for election, and in many other ways were in sympathy with the men of the county and their large families, we should not expect all laws to be rigidly enforced, especially one so seemingly unjust and exorbitant as the whisky tax.

With this state of affairs prevailing in most mountain counties, the Prohibition Amendment was passed in 1918. The burden of enforcement was now shifted to the federal government. The smallest unit of federal government became the state district, comprising several counties. The staff was extremely small, made up of a judge and a district marshal or two. The marshal had authority to ask for help from county officers. When a marshal had evidence of whisky making in a county (from reports and confessions made by bootleggers and drunks), he organized a "raid" for a county and called on the sheriff and constables for help.

Now we can see how Jim and Dave could make whisky for many years and almost never be molested, never be arrested, and therefore never be involved in killing and being killed. The constables of their districts often sent them word beforehand of an organized raid. The men set watches and prepared to get away from the vicinity of a still, always taking the most valuable items (worms and other hardware) and the most damning evidence (whisky and personal belongings). When the officers came upon a still, they could not make any arrests, but they always carried with them pickaxes and hammers. With these they proceeded to smash the jugs and fruitjars, pour out the barrels of mash and cut the hoops off the barrels, and stave pick holes in the cooker, still, and other vessels.

No two raiding parties were ever alike, I suppose, but they varied between two extremes, from orderly to violent, depending largely upon the marshal and his attitude. The distillers as a rule had but one desire, and that was to escape arrest. The story of the little boy who, when offered fifty cents to tell where his parents were, asked for the money in advance and explained by saying, "If you go up there, you ain't coming back," is highly exaggerated. Most men at a still, though they carried guns, did not want the crime of murder upon them.

Some marshals conducted orderly raids into mountain counties. They were aware of the fact that they had an unpopular and almost impossible law to enforce. Some were human enough to know that the county officials sympathized with an old farmer (sincere, honest, law-abiding in every way except moonshining) who had a large family and very little income to support them. The marshals knew also that hunting a lawbreaker did not give them the right to commit murder. Thus, when the officers made their approach on a still in some dark hollow, the rule of conduct was to arrest the operators if they were present and arrestable. But if one had a fair start in the other direction, he was not their man and should not be shot unlawfully in the back. If he were identified, he could be arrested later and handled by due process of law.

On the other hand, some marshals might be out to get their man, or the county officials might have political or personal scores to settle. The raiding party would go armed with Winchesters and pistols, and steal upon the scene from all sides. They would accost the still operator with threats and shouts. Upon one involuntary move on his part the armed men would riddle his body with bullets. Many men in the mountains thus have been shot down in violent and unlawful ways. The officers can easily say, and usually do say, that the man resisted arrest, or offered violence, or attempted to run from the scene of an illicit still. But no matter what the alibi given for such a crime, the entire citizenry of the county is so shocked by such a sordid murder that they tend to show less respect for law and its brutal enforcement.

When Jim Couch said that he made whisky to pay his taxes and buy food and clothing, he was giving his side as he saw it.

He and Dave made whisky through the 1930's because there was almost no other source of income. The fact that they and others do not make it now is a sign of the times. The Second World War brought many changes. With it came a revival of mining, lumbering, and other industries. Moonshining among the Couches and over the whole region almost ceased, because the people had easier, more honorable, and better paying jobs for supporting their families.

CHAPTER 5

DAVE AND JIM, THEIR FOLKWAYS

"ONCET my grandfather was a-thrashing wheat in the cove," Dave began when I started the recorder for a session of pioneer legends, "and he heared a hog squealing 'way up towards the top of the hill under a clift. He was thrashing that wheat with a big frailpole, what they allas used for it. He just laid his pole on his shoulder and broke in a run up the side of the mountain to find out what was wrong with his hog. Got up there, and they was a bear had it hugged right up in its arms a-gnawing it in the top of the head. He lit in on that bear with his frailpole, and he beat that bear to death before it would turn the hog loose. He took the bear in and skinned him and had him a good warm bearhide and some meat.

"He went again into the woods, him and his boys, and they holded a bear in the holler of an old chestnut tree. They was a hole went in just above the top of the ground, and the bear went in there. The dogs pushed right on in on it, and they fit the bear till they finally killed it. It had hurt a dog so bad they had to go on and leave the dog there. So they skinned the bear and took the hide and all the meat they could carry and went on.

"It got late on 'em, and they decided to lay out under a clift that night. They had 'em some of that bear meat br'iled for supper, and then they laid down. In that day and time the painters [panthers] were so thick you couldn't hardly do nothing like handle fresh meat in the hills for 'em; they would come to you and try to take it. A whole gang of them painters surrounded that clift that night, coming up, trying to get at that bear meat. Grandpa said he'd throw great chunks of far at them painters and scatter 'em off down the hill. They [Dave often pronounced *they* with a long *e*] had to fight them painters all night to keep 'em from coming in and taking their bear meat and maybe hurting somebody. Fit 'em off with far chunks.

"An old bear got to using around clost to my grandpa's house one time. He had some bee gums, and they would try to tear into them and rob 'em. Well, he thought he'd set a trap for that old bear. He got a trough and took him out about a half a gallon of honey from a gum and got about a quart of moonshine whisky. He mixed the two up and poured it all into that trough. Went out there next morning and saw he had that old bear. There he was—laying drunk. He was just laying there flat on his back playing with his feet. Grandpa shot his brains out and got him another pile of meat and a good bearhide.

"This is another true bear story, and it goes back to my mother's grandfather. His wife went to her neighbor's house, about a mile and a half from one house to the other. People was thin settled in that day and time, and they was plenty of bear. She was there with her baby four months old and had to start back home. There was some clivves on the way. And the clift on one side of her was close, and they was a big bear a-laying out under there. As she passed, why it retch out and bit her little baby's head off and swallered it. She had to go on in home crying with the rest of her baby. And the old man he got him another man or two and went and killed the bear and cut it open and got the little baby's head back. They buried it with the baby. Now that was a true story, happened over there on Greasy Creek.

"My mother was borned and raised in Harlan County and my father in Perry County. When they married, they settled down over there in the Sang Branch. There wasn't very many bear and deer at that time—about all had scattered off and left. But anyhow, down in the Dollar Branch of Greasy some feller had a cornfield and something got to using in it, and it come out to be an old she-bear and her one little cub. They got out to hunting for these bears—my father, Ed Barnes, Will Minyard, John Huff, Willis Turner—they was a whole passel of 'em started hunting. And they all had their favorite dogs—my father had one he called Punk and another he called Nigger. They bayed up in a swag, and when they got up clost, they thought the dogs had cornered a gang of hogs. When they went in on 'em, the bears commenced to running ever which way, and the men follered their dogs after a bear. Some of the men went to the top of the ridge so they could get a shot at one if he crossed the point.

"My dad's and Tom Harris's dogs treed out on a flat, and when they got there they was barking up an old crooked water-oak. Up in that tree was an old bear behind some water sprouts, just hunkered down up there like somebody would. Come to find out they never had a gun, and Tom had nothing but an old thirty-two bulldog pistol, and it was so old it throwed the balls crossways. Tom up with that old pistol two shots and never tipped the bear. He just had one shot left. Dad said he got the gun from Tom and with that last shot he hit that bear right between the eyes. That old bear just sunk down, and they didn't know if they had killed him or not.

"Said they watched him around there for a little while, but he never would fall out of the tree. Dad said he pulled off his shoes and skinned that tree to kick the bear out. About the time he got up in there, why, here come another old bear right through there, scared Tom away because he didn't have no gun. And said that old bear stopped at the roots of the tree and looked up in it, and if it hadn't been for the dogs pressing him by now, he might have come up in there. Guess that was one time dad was betwixt a rock and a hard place.

"He kicked that old bear out of there and give chase to the other un. It run through Alex's Branch and got old Lewis Turner after it with an old muzzle-loading shotgun loaded with rifle bullets. They chased it from there into Rockhouse Branch of Greasy and back into Alex's Branch. Dad said they could have killed it a dozen times if they hadn't been afeared to kill the dogs. Will Minyard had a dog a-hanging right onto the old bear's jaw most of the time. Willis Turner got holt of that old muzzle-loader and cracked down at it. Well, he killed the bear and the dog too. It made Will so mad he wouldn't let Willis have nary bite of that bear meat.

"Purty soon they was all after another old big un, and run it plumb into Dollar Branch. Rob Turner lived up in there and got after it, and he didn't have no gun, only an old forty-four cap-and-ball pistol. He caught up with it and run it out of Dollar Branch into Greasy Creek and waded the water right by its side. He snapped his pistol six times right into that bear's head, and that gun wouldn't go off. That bear got away from them.

"One time my mother went to stay with her granny while the old man was gone. They lived in a log house, and for protection he had built a palin' fence around the yard about four feet high. A bear come that night and got inside that palin'. The dog barked at something all night, but the old lady was scared to get up and see what it was. Next morning there was a big bear right in the yard. It would start to climb them palin's, and the dog would grab it by the rump and it'd have to jump back on the dog. He had kept that up all night. My grandmother got the rifle-gun and killed it. That made one she killed. They allas skinned them bear and stocked up on meat for the winter. Dry the meat out like we allas do hog meat and eat it. They say bear meat was awful good. They would sell the hides or make shoes out of 'em. They made what they called moccasins. That was about all the kind of shoes they had back in my grandma's raising up.

"When my mother was just a little girl, deers was purty frequent in that country. One day the dogs got after a deer and run it right into a big hole of water below her house. The menfolks was all out hunting down to the mouth of Greasy. And mother said her mother said for her to go down there on a rock over the waterhole and see if she could see a way to get that deer. She said she went down there and got on that rock.

The old deer kept swimming around and around in there. And one time when it come around under that ledge of rock, why, she just hauled off and jumped right astraddle of its neck, took it to the bottom, and helt it there till it drownded.

"I don't know about telling this un or not. Some men was hunting in Abner's Branch one time, trying to get after some bear that was using in there. They hunted all day, and the dogs was running bear and deer all over the place. One run a deer out of there and plumb out to the mouth of the branch and right across the road. Old Rock Minyard was going along the road at that time, and when that deer started up the hill away from him, he cracked down and killed that deer and never even busted the hide on it nowhere. He hit it right in the center of the bunghole."

Dave went into his pocket after his crooked briar pipe, letting me understand that his pioneering legends were exhausted. But I knew he had more, especially some old yarns about the Civil War. These I requested after he had had a good smoke.

"Well, back in the old Civil War my grandfather John Couch was a soldier, and he used to tell us boys about their ventures with the Rebels and how they fit 'em. Said one time him and a bunch of men knowed the Rebels was a-coming over a certain path, and they waylaid 'em on the top of a clift. They come riding along, and one of the Rebels in front was carrying a flag, a Rebel flag. They all picked 'em out a man to shoot offen his horse. Said he picked the flagsman. They come riding along, and they cracked down on 'em with their muskets. Killed sebem or eight of them. The rest of the Rebels jumped off their horses and took atter 'em.

"Run 'em all over the hills and plumb to the top of the mountain. Said he got away and run on till he got so hot he couldn't go no further. He rolled over behind a big chestnut log to rest. Said they got so clost on him he could hear 'em a-getting their breath—they come so nigh a-getting him.

"The next battle they had was over around Big Stone Gap, Virginia. They run into the Rebels over there, and the Rebels got too hot for them and scattered 'em. Captured one of my grandmother's brothers. My grandfather and another one of my great-uncles got away. Said they come back toward Lynch there on the Virginia side of the mountain and set there all night. He had got separated from my great-uncle and didn't know where nobody was at. Next morning, time day got to breaking, he could hear something thrashing in the sticks out from him. He got to peeping around, with his old musket ready to kill it. Thought it was a Rebel. When he spied it, it turned out to be Uncle Hen Shepherd. Said they had set in about thirty foot of one another all night and didn't know one another was there that clost.

"Old man Arie Shepherd got captured, but he begin to try his best to get away before they took him off somewhere to prison. The Rebels had a lot of sheep gathered up where they had driven them off from the people's fields for the last few days. Arie got down amongst their sheep in a lot there, and he would baa like a sheep and move around in them till he found a way to get out and ex-cape the guards around their camp. Finally he saw his chance, and he broke through and run. Thought they was after him, and he run across that Black Mountain and run plumb on in home on Big Leatherwood. And he was so hot and give out, he laid down and never got up again. Laid there and died, he had got so overheated.

"The Rebels come through the Greasy Creek country. And they surrounded the home of old man Alex Turner's. Robbed him, took what he had, all the grub he had to eat. Then they all told him they wanted his gun. He told 'em he never had no gun. They got to searching and hunting all over the place, and finally found his old hog rifle—hid betwixt the feather bed and straw bed. They took it and started off with him too. Said they were going to kill him. His wife follered 'em with their babies and cried and bagged. And finally they turned him loose.

"That's about all I know of the Civil War stories. People don't tell them old legends much any more, and I've about forgot the most of them. But I used to hear them from just

about anybody around where I growed up, and they could
make them things sound so scary and dangerous the hair would
stand up on my head. It was mostly the women and the old men
who was left in here to take care of theirselves. Nearly everybody in here was called Republicans; that means they was for
Lincoln and the North. But just any bunch o' soldiers passing
through would want to take everything they seen. People had
to hide out their cattle and horses—take 'em to the woods and
tie 'em up—had to hide out their belongings like guns and
quilts and tools, dig holes in the gyardens or in the stalls of
their barns, and bury 'em. They would hide their meat and
cans of lard in holes under the floor or just anywhere to preserve
it. And every man that could carry a gun was allas under
suspicion. If the Rebels couldn't get a man to go with 'em to
join their forces, they would be just as apt to hang him as anything else. When my mother's father was still under age, he
was laid under suspicion, and for the last year of the war he
laid out under a clift and let the folks slip food to him of a
night to keep 'em from taking him out of here.

"I guess you have heared about Rebel Rock up here on the
road crossing Pine Mountain. I can tell ye about how that
happened, but they are several ideas about the details of it.
They was a bunch of Union soldiers come up through the Pore
Fork here looking for Rebels that would slip over here from
Virginia and make raids on the people and carry off their food
stuff and drive off their cattle. They run into a purty good
sized detachment of the Rebels right in here. They went to
fighting and shooting one another, and the Union boys got the
best of the other side and put 'em on the run. And naturally
they took to the hills. If you have ever noticed, you see the
rocks and ridges in the Pine Mountain stick out up the hill
and not down it. The Rebels broke into groups, ever' man for
hisself, and about three of 'em took up the spur of the point and
some Union soldiers right after 'em. They come up to the
upper end of that spur and couldn't get no further. They was
cornered on the edge of that clift, about seventy-five feet high.

They had to turn and fight and risk being killed, or jump off
that high clift and take their chances. Two of the Rebels turned
and tried to shoot their way back down the spur, but they got
killed and the Union men throwed the corpses off. The other
man thought he could make it off 'cause they was a purty good
sized fir tree just off the clift and retch up nearly to the top.
He jumped into that tree, and as luck would have it, he landed
in the top limbs and skinned down and got away. They say the
frames of them dead Rebels laid up there in the crevices till the
meat dropped offen their frames. Nobody would take a chance
to bury 'em, afeared somebody would think they favored the
other side."

Dave became quiet and reached for his pipe, a signal for me to
stop the recorder. Some of the interesting pioneering folktales
that he told during this and other sessions were Indian Binge,
We Killed a Bear, and Seven Dead Indians [microcard ed., Nos.
52, 53, 51; see also Chapter 6].

Jim had begun to show a great deal of interest in this collecting project, especially after I came back from Georgia in
1954 and pursued him to help me get a complete sampling of
the family's lore. I had become increasingly aware of the ex-
haustless nature of a family's traditions. Since Jim believed in
remedies and practiced bloodstopping, I let him talk at some
length on these two folkways.

"I am going to tell you a whole string of witchcrafts," Jim
said as he settled down to recording, "that happened up and
down Cutshin and Greasy creeks, and most of them I saw with
my own eyes.

"One of my great-great-uncles was named Mat Layson [fic-
titious], and he was a witch. His brother had a boy named
Henry, and he told me this happened to him. Old Mat taken
him out one time to train him to be a witch. Well, Henry said
he took him out one morning just as the sun was rising over
the hill. Said he set a silver plate he had down on the ground
behind him. He cursed the Lord and blessed the Devil and

then shot at the sunball. Said he farred three shots, and every time he would shoot, a drop of clear blood would fall in that silver plate behind him.

"He told Henry, 'Now put your hand on top of your head and the other'n at the bottom of your feet. Now swear that you'll give all between those hands to the Devil to do with you just as he pleases.' Henry, being a boy, did what he told him. Old Mat said, 'Now we'll go right over to the old lick and kill us a deer.'

"Well, Henry said he went on over to the old lick with him, and he told him to be quiet. Said Mat said some kind of ceremony and made some kind of noise, and the deer was coming through there just like a gang of sheep. He ra'red up and said, 'Lord how mercy!' and when he said that, they just vanished and were gone. The old man cussed him out and told him never to say that again. He told him he wouldn't.

"They went on up to the top of another ridge, and old Mat said, 'Now we are going to kill us a turkey.' He said his ceremony again and some talking, and he said forty or fifty big turkeys flew in there and flopped right down and lit all over the ground around them. He said he just ra'red up again and said, 'Lord how mercy!' He said when he said that, all the turkeys disappeared.

"He said old Mat told him, 'For a little I'd kill you right here. You don't know how to be a witch.' Uncle Henry said he was afraid to tell that for a long time after, afraid he would die.

"Weren't long after that old Mat went to Henry Shepherd's father's house to try and get some milk. And they told him they didn't have milk to spare. Just enough for the fambly. Well, in a little while it got so their cows wouldn't give no milk. They'd just run into the gap a-bawling and bawling and cutting a shine. They wouldn't give no milk. They got to inquiring about it, and they found an old feller over there who was a kind of witch doctor, and he told Henry's mother that a man would come there between this time and tomor' night. Says, 'Don't you let him have a thing offen this place. Don't even let him have a drink of water.' He said, 'If you don't, your cows will be all right and never be bothered again.' Well, the next day she looked out and saw the old man Mat a-coming. Said he come over and set around a few minutes, and he asked her to let him borrey some salt. She told him that she didn't have it. And he asked her to let him borrey some coffee, and she said she didn't have that. Everything he would ask for, she would tell him she didn't have it. He said, 'I believe I want a drink of water.' And she said, 'They hain't a drop of water in the house.' He went out and got that water bucket and took the dipper and turned it up and drained the water bucket enough to get him a swaller of water before he left there.

"Another time old Mat showed his witchcrafts. Back in Leatherwood in Perry County it was awful thin settled in there and in Greasy and along the Harlan County line. An old man there by the name of Ransom Turner nearly allas kept a bunch of dogs. And they would get over on Big Laurel Creek and in that section and jump a deer and bring it over to Leatherwood, and then they would lose it in the creek where old Mat lived.

"Uncle Henry said one time he heared the dogs coming down the old House Branch of Leatherwood and said his daddy jumped on a horse and took down the creek lickety-split to see what they's after. They was a big waterhole there on Leatherwood. The deers when they got run in there they would generally run in that waterhole for protection from the dogs. He rode his horse like a ball of far down there. Got purty close to the place, and he saw the deer come in across the road. And all at once the dogs turned right back the other way, just bawling every breath in their back tracks. Said he rode a few paces further where a hornbean bush growed right next to the small creek. He stopped and saw old Mat right in the top of that hornbean bush just a-wringing and twisting and a-tying them limbs in knots, and them dogs every one turning on the back track. He said the ugliest word he ever heared his daddy say in his life he said right then. He said he looked up at old

Mat and said, 'Mat, if they was no hell and if I had a gun, damned if I didn't kill you, you old turkey cock.'

"His daddy went to the waterhole and got him a deer anyway. You see, old Mat witched the dogs and turned them on their back tracks toward home soon as the deer run off in there, so's he could get the deer. But they had seen the dogs after them and saw the deer run to the waterhole this time and got their deer.

"That's all I care to tell on Mat Layson, but they was another old feller down there on Greasy Creek name of Charles Isaacs [fictitious] who was a witch and a doctor and a preacher all in one. I have heared different people tell about his witchcrafts, and some instances I know are true because I saw them myself. I was coming from Hyden one time, me and a man by the name of Carter Turner. And old Ike Whitaker they called him lived at the mouth of Maggard's Branch. It got up in the night, and me and Carter put up to stay all night with him. He was Carter's uncle, and old Charles was there. Carter had a dog that he bought off of Coon Creek and had him chained with a chain, and we tied him to the palin' fence outside of the house.

"We was setting around and weren't noticing Charles too much. He was an old funny feller. He raised up and said, 'If I'm not mistaken, your dog is loose.' Well, Carter got up and we went out and, sure enough, the dog was loose. We put the chain back around the dog's neck and wired it with a wire, and it was impossible for the dog to get loose.

"We went back in and was setting there talking, and in about thirty minutes old Charles said, 'Your dog is loose again.' We started up and got on the outside of the door, and I told Carter, said, 'You know he told a lie.' We went out there, and that old dog was loose again. We just tied him back up and went in again.

"Set around a few more minutes. Now old Ike Whitaker never had a chicken on the place. Charles raised up and started talking about chickens. Ike said, 'I hain't got a chicken on the place.' 'Why, I know you have,' Charles said. Ike said, 'I know

I hain't.' Old Charles slapped his leg and crowed right big. An old rooster under the floor r'ared up and crowed just as big as you please. Ike said they weren't a chicken on that place.

"I have heared a dozen suchlike incidents on him. Old Charles had all of his cattle named. He'd go out in the yard, and if he wanted one of his cattle in, ever which one he wanted in from the field to the house, he would call its name, and that thing would throw its tail over its back and it never stopped till it got there, bawling ever' breath. He had a big gang of hogs. Other people had hogs that run right along with his'n. And he'd go out and feed his hogs, and nobody else's hogs wouldn't take a bite.

"Another thing I saw him do one time with my own eyes. I was down on Cutshin one time at a man's house, and we's out in the cornfield, big bottom of corn waist high. Old Charles rode up and rode right out into that cornfield, set down, and turned his horse loose among that corn. I was wondering if that old horse wouldn't start eating that corn. Nobody never said nothing, and Charles said that old horse could stay in there a month and he'd never crack a blade nor he wouldn't step on none. That old horse picked on around there as long as I stayed. If he ever cracked a blade, I never saw it, and he never would step on a hill of corn.

"Old Charles peddled all the time, and he would stop at people's houses and sometimes show 'em what he could do. They would go out in the barnyard, and if they was a sheep there, he would tell it to butt the chimley, and it would draw back and butt that chimley with all power. He'd flop his arms and crow like a rooster, and ever' rooster on the place would start crowing. He witched a man's cow one time and got it to walk up a ladder into the barn loft, and they liked to never got it outten there again. He would doctor the people and take warts and wens offen them ever'where he went. He had some kind of religious beliefs, and one time he took a notion to sacrifice his son. He dug a big hole in the gyarden and put some logs and chunks in there and some far, and had his son get

down in there and lay down on them burning logs. It weren't
burning to do no good, and he went back in the house for
another shovelful of far, and the boy jumped out of there and
run off.

"What caused old Charles to die, he had a wen to come on
his side and he operated on it. It set up gangerine [gangrene],
and he died from it. He was a man that could do without sleep
all the time, I have heared tell. They said that he never aver-
aged more than four hours' sleep of a night. My brother-in-law
tells this on him. He was with Charles one time, and they was
talking about going hunting. And all at once a big fine dog
run right by him and took up the hill. Charles weren't to be
seen anywheres. That dog went up the hill and treed a coon
and got up in that tree some way and caught it. By the time
my brother-in-law got there, it was back down on the ground,
and then it turned itself back into a man and there stood old
Charles. Now who would believe a tale like that? I have
heared my brother-in-law tell that time and again. I don't recollect another like that.

"They was an old feller there on Greasy Creek name of Ed
Horner [fictitious] that ever'body called a witch. Them fellers
that lived over there allas had dogs, and they hunted coons a
lot, you know. They'd take their dogs and see who had the
best one. They'd get out a coon hunting, and old Ed would
spell their dogs, they called it, and make them bark up trees
and weren't nothing in 'em. On one occasion they went hunting
back in Gabe's Branch in there in the wilderness. Said their
dogs run about an hour and treed, and they went to 'em and
said they got up there to them and something flew out of that
tree went like a load of chains and everything. They allas
called it the devil flew out. They got to where they couldn't
catch nothing with their dogs. A man by the name of Jake
Howard lived over there on Baxter claimed he was a repeller, a
feller that could turn your tricks on you. They went over to
Jake's and told him about their dogs, told him Ed was spelling
their dogs and their dogs weren't no 'count. Old Jake asked

them, 'Now just what do you want done to him? Do you want him killed?' They said, 'No, we don't want him killed.' 'Well,' he said, 'what about putting one of his eyes out—do you reckon that would help him?' They finally agreed to have Ed's eye put out. Well, they come on back home and their dogs was all right, and Ed had one eye from then on. I knowed him well.

"They said he would go to their matches where they used to have these old hog-rifle shooting matches, and he would get around and tell them fellers, 'Well, your gun won't far this time.' They'd crack down and their cap would bust, but their gun wouldn't go off. They would start putting powder in the tubes of their guns. He'd take his knife out and open it and put it back between his lags and say it wouldn't shoot, and when he would take it out and say, 'Now your gun is all right if you will far.' I don't know how he done it. He'd hold his knife back between his legs and tell them their gun wouldn't far, and shore enough it wouldn't. Then he'd take it out and tell them it would far, and she would far off so clear and purty.

"My mother told me one time when she was just a small girl a bunch of people lived in there on Greasy Creek by the name of Yates, and there was one widder woman named Hester. Said ever' time she would pass, she would want them girls, her and her sister, to go up in Rockhouse Branch and stay all night with her. Then one night her mother finally agreed to let 'em go. Said they went up there, and they done up the work. Getting supper, and the old lady never had a cow on the place. Said she told them, 'Well, I'll churn and we'll have supper ready.' She grabbed the old churn and the dishrag, and right behind the door she went. Said she stayed in there about five minutes, and she come out of there with the awfulest bowl of butter that she had taken out of that churn. She knowed she didn't have no cow, but she didn't know where she got that butter. Of course they are a lot of these things.

"They was another feller over there called old man Saw Adams. They called him a charm doctor. I have seen his miracles work. My dad had a wen, they called it, on his kneecap one time, and it was about the size of a good-sized goose egg. He went to the regular doctors with it. They claimed they would have to pull it out, take it off—operate on it. He was passing one day, and he heared about how Uncle Saw Adams was a charm doctor. He was hoeing corn out in the field, and my dad just rode up and hollered out at him. Talking to him, and then Uncle Saw said to him, 'Pull your britches lag up and let me take a look at it.' He pulled his britches lag up, and he looked at it from over in the field away from it. Told him to go on. In three days there weren't a sign of a scratch on him where that wen was. That was charm. These charms is true, because I can do 'em myself. It's a secret and can't be told. If I was to tell you my secret, then it would be no good to me. I learned it from my mother. It's bloodstopping."

I said, "Maybe you should tell us about your herb remedies and then finish up with your secret bloodstopping cure."

"Well, when I was growing up, they weren't no chance to get a regular doctor to the house when you needed him. Never but one doctor inside our house that I can remember of until I got grown. My mother would gather different things in the mountains just according to how you was sick. If you had the old grips, we called it, and what the fancy doctors called pneumonia, we would go to the fields with mother, and she would gather stuff that she called horsemint, wintergreen, hornbean bark, and pine top, and boil that all together and make a tea out of it. When that don't break up a fever on you, brother, you might just as well quit.

"We never did have no colds to speak of in them days, and not near the diseases people have now'days. For colds and stuff we had nothing but quinine and calamy we bought at the drugstores. They called it Sagame Calamy, in powder form. A dose was what you could get out on the point of a knife. For croup we used groundhog grease or coal oil for a medicine for that. Now if one had the misfortune of catching something like the eetch, she would take this old pokeroot and make a ooze out of it and boil it and wash you with it and kill that eetch dead as a nit, buddy. We used gunpowder for the sore mouth and salt water for the eyes.

"We used a medicine called sweet oil for the yearache. My dad got it over in Virginia. Virginia Lee I think he called it. He would put that ooze in our years to take care of a yearache. For any kind of stomach trouble or disorder we would drink sody water or vinegar. For a running off of the bowels we had three or four remedies. Most of the time we would go out and dig us some blackberry roots, steam and heat 'em, and make a syrup out of that. Make a starch out of flour sometimes. But you know when I was growing up, you didn't see much of that running off 'cause people eat hard foods all the time such as milk, butter, meat, cabbage, and beans, stuff like that. People weren't sick not one-third of the time like they are now'days.

"Another thing for the sick stomach—we would allas try to throw up and get it offen our stomachs. We would take a little whisky out in a pan and set it afar and burn it down to a black scum and drink the results of that. It was an awful funny tasting stuff, and I've drunk a lot of it. For the cramps, stomach ache or belly ache, take gunpowder and mix it with cold water and throw it up off your stomach. Another thing was hookle berries —not huckleberries you know in the hills. This grows up like a sunflower and have a head on 'em. I ain't seen any in a long time. They'd grow in the gyarden. Two things for a snakebite was whisky and what they called Japanese oil. Both good for snakebite. My dad got a bottle of Japanese oil one time when my brother got snake-bit. He couldn't get the seal cap off the top. Couldn't get it off, and he jobbed the stopper down in there, and the stuff flew and hit him in the eye, and it come in a hair causing him to go blind, when that strong medicine hit him in the eye.

"Now this bloodstopping remedy I was telling you about, I learnt it from my mother. I don't know where she come into possession of it, but they can't but one know it in the fambly. I can tell it to my fambly, but I can't never operate it no more. It's a bloodstopping method. I have tried it, and it works.

I tried it up on Leatherwood one time, and an old preacher and them made fun of me. We was working together, and I was talking about it to some fellers, and about that time my brother got a piece of steel in his hand. The blood was streaming off his hand just as big as it could stream, running off his fingers, where he had cut the artery in the top of his hand. He come up and said, 'Lord how mercy, do something to stop it.' I said, 'Don't you touch it!' I told my brother, I said, 'You walk off the top of the hill and set down on that log.' He walked off and set down on that log, and in about ten minutes it stopped and cleared up. That old preacher told me, said, 'It just quit itself—you never done it. You're not a Christian, and you can't work miracles like that.' I said, 'It's not a miracle—it's only a charm.'

"Passed on a week or two, and they's a Campbell boy there had his nose bust and was bleeding him to death, already had him bleeded so weak he couldn't hardly walk. I come in from work about four o'clock. That Campbell boy's nose had been bleeding since about two o'clock. It went on till about five-thirty. Couldn't get nobody to take him out of there to Hazard to the doctor. This Holiness preacher was there, and all the men that worked there. I said, 'Uncle Jason, you don't believe what I's telling you.' I said, 'If you was to see something happen, would you believe it?' He said, 'I certainly would.' I called the boy out of the washroom, where he was holding his head with a washcloth with his nose bleeding. I hollered and said, 'Straighten up.' I said, 'Turn around.' He turned around. I said, 'Uncle Jason, do you see any blood?' He said, 'No.' I said, 'Do you believe it now?' He said, 'Yes.' That was Uncle Jason Smith.

"Another time I was coming home from work over there, and Rile Hendrix had a wife that something had happened to her. They called it the flux. Had a doctor with her two or three times, and he hadn't done her no good. Rile told me, come out in the road and stopped me, and we was talking. I said, 'Rile, I never had an experience of a thing like that, but I'll do what

I can.' I put on my charm. While we was there, before I left, his wife come to the door. She come out there and said, 'You know, I'm all right now.' Rile told me she had been that way for about two days.

"Then my time come in 1918 in the World War. I don't doubt if I didn't save a thousand lives. Boys would get wounded in the war and be bleeding bad. I'd do all the same; if I got a German, I'd administrate with him the same as I would with the Americans. It can be done, and don't let nobody tell you it can't be. If nobody don't believe it, come to me and I'll show 'em that it can be.

"It is a charm and can't be used for nothing but to stop blood. It's handed down from the Old Testament in the Bible. It has come from Ezekiel. I've knowed members of other famblies that could do it too. There was an old man by the name of Jim Koontz could do it, 'cause he performed it on me. I know it worked.

"I fell off a train one time when I was small and stuck a stake in my face, and my nose bled me so weak I couldn't get to my feet. Weren't a chance to get a doctor. Jim Koontz lived about a mile away, and the saying was that Jim could stop blood. Well, when my dad come in from work, he sent another boy just as hard as he could go to Jim Koontz. When he got there, he said Jim said, the first word was, 'Has his nose bled long?' He told him yeaw, he didn't know how long though. He said, 'Well, he's wet his head.' That boy told him he didn't know whether I had or not. But by the time that boy got to Jim Koontz, my nose had never bled another drop. My nose hain't bled since that time I don't guess a half a teacupful.

"Then another man I can prove I 'formed the charm on is old man Hampton Turner. His boy came to me about one o'clock in the night and said his dad had a cat-tar in his head, he called it. The doctors claimed, or the nurse—they didn't have no doctors then—his nose was bleeding out of both nose-holes just about as free as it could bleed. The boy stopped in the middle of the road and hollered me up and wanted me to come down there. I said, 'What's the matter?' He said, 'Pap's nose is a-bleeding him to death.' I said, 'It's no sech a thing.' He said, 'It is; it's a-bleeding him to death.' I said, 'I bet you his nose hain't bleeding a drop.' I jerked my clothes on, tore out, and went to the house. When I got there, the old man's nose wa'n't bleeding a drop."

Jim came to a halt as if he had proved his point and there was nothing else to record. I asked him about the mystery of the charm, if it took faith, if he said words, or if he just thought of something. All he would say was that it could not be divulged without losing it, and he finally quieted me and finished the session by saying, "Well, I can't explore it no further with you."

CHAPTER 6

THE COUCHES' TALES AND SONGS

IT WAS storytelling and folksinging, of course, which first led me to the Couch family and the interviews that grew into a study of the whole way of life of a mountain family. The quality and quantity of stories and songs I have collected from the family are surprising, although I now know that I have not yet exhausted the store and perhaps never can. Jim said to me once when I was looking for a time to wind up the collecting and start transcribing and editing the lore: "Why, you hain't near collected all the stuff from us 'cause we've about forgot all of it. I bet you you don't have not one third of the songs we have knowed since pap started pickin' and singin' back yander before he's married." At that time I was approaching an even hundred songs recorded from Jim and Dave alone and about sixty of the longer traditional stories.

During each session, while the performers stopped to smoke and chat, I made it a point to ask them about times and places for songs to be sung and tales to be told by the old folk of the family. Any time or place was suitable, they replied, but there were favorite occasions, of course. Once in reply Dave said, "My parents would call us in the house and tell us riddles or yarns till along up in the night. That would get us in the big house [living room] and draw us together. It's got so in these days and times they can't get their chillern together long enough to have any fun. People hain't interested enough to tell 'em tales. They are all the time out and into something.

"I can't say they was any set time for any kind of thing. It would be just what my daddy got started on, and if it suited her, my mother would give us a story or two. They would set and tell mostly of a night, tell half the night, or till we got sleepy and went to bed. My daddy didn't know as many stories as mother, but he would take off on a bear tale, or something about the Civil War, or have his old banjer down picking around on it and sing a few songs. We would set and listen—a lot of enjoyment in the home all the time. Mother would generally tell her stories of a night, when she got through with her jobs, got all the work done and seen that everything was ready for morning. We would set around the far, and she would come in and get to knitting or cutting out a quilt pattern, and we would get after her to tell us a story. She didn't mind telling a giant story or about something that happened to her and her people 'way back yander. She was allas good and kind to us, took an interest in us and kept us all together. We would set up all night and listen if she would go on. But she would have to stop and carry one of the little uns to bed, and then she would think about the morning's work and make us hit the feathers. She would allas put us to bed early of a summertime because we would have to work in the corn or in the woods."

Jim had this to say about storytelling. "If my mother was just entertaining us kids in the yard of a summer evening, or around the far of a night, she would tell us some mild fireside story. But if she wanted to scare us, or we wanted scared, she would get into them ghost and witch tales. And if we had company around, just us men would go into them big tall tales and funny Arshman jokes. Maybe wind up a-telling riddles and solving puzzles. Just anything to have a big time.

"My people have allas been a riddling fambly. I can't remember when I didn't know a lot o' them, and we would tell 'em any time we took a notion around the far at night. And then they was allas good to try on strangers when we had somebody staying all night with us.

"I can tell you a time when I learnt the most riddles and when we told 'em the most. One time we lived right clost to a

sawmill set. My daddy was working at the mill, and my mother took four or five of the men in to board. The men was allas trying to pull a joke on one another, and playing pranks. And they got onto riddling. My daddy knowed about as many as the rest of the boys. Sometimes at night they would set out on a log and swap riddles till bedtime. They wouldn't tell the answers, just leave the fellers to study 'em out. They would run into one another next day or sometime and try to onriddle one they had heared. And they ever'one had some puzzles and riddles on one another. Of course the feller who had a riddle out that nobody could do a thing with, he was the champeen for a while.

"My daddy learnt a lot of new riddles that way, and we little fellers heared 'em too and would tell 'em to our playmates. Then we would say 'em over again at night to visitors and guests long atter that job had worked out and the mill was moved. Why, I've told riddles out a-hunting or riding with somebody horseback to town, or we would have a few at the ends of corn rows when we worked in the fields. I guess we done more riddling in the fambly than anything else, at times we did."

These are some of the general remarks made by the tellers of tales. They had other, more particular, comments for each of the stories. These will be appended to some of the representative stories to follow.

These stories were taken down almost without exception by tape recorder. I have done the very minimum of editing, and that editing has been to make the tales more readable on the printed page. No stories have been combined, enlarged, or in any way rewritten for this purpose. They are included here as they were told to me. The first one is the delightful story told by Bobby McDaniel. The folklorist will recognize it as one of the several versions of Type 480, which in the Grimm collection is "Mother Holle." It is No. 2 in the microcard edition. Mandy, you will remember, would not tell stories any more, and she said she guessed Jim had told this one to Bobby. But Jim did not know it so well and felt sure Mandy had told it to Bobby; and if this is true, Mandy was indulging in storytelling up until almost the time I found her over in Leslie County. Bobby called it

THE TWO GALS

Once upon a time there was a man who married, and him and his old woman had a purty gal. The old woman died, and the man married again. This time they had an ugly gal. The stepmother was mean to the purty gal and made her do all the work, and she was good to her gal and let her set around and play with her purties. One day the old woman sent the purty gal to the well to draw a bucket of drinking water. The bucket was so heavy she couldn't hardly draw it up, and she slipped and fell in the well. And when she come to the bottom, she raised up and saw she was in another world.

She got up and started walking down the road to see where it went to and what and all she could see down there. And she come to a big log acrost the road. Hit was holler, and she heared it say, "Go around me, little gal," and she went around it.

Then she come to an apple tree just a-hanging full of purty red apples and she wanted some. When she started to get some, the apple tree said, "Climb me and get all the apples you want, but don't break any of my sprouts."

She never broke no sprouts. Got her some apples and went on. She come to a cow, and that cow needed milking. She said, "Milk me, milk me, little gal. Get all the milk you want and hang the bucket back on my horns."

She milked the cow and got all the milk she could drink and hung the bucket back on her horns. And then she come to a sheep, and it was just as woolly as it could be. It said, "Shear me, shear me, little gal, and get all the wool you want and hang the shears back on my horns."

She sheared the sheep and took some of the wool and hung

the shears back on its horns. She went on along the road and come to a house. A witch lived there, but the gal didn't know it. She asked the woman if she could get a job of work with her. The witch said, "Yes, but you have to rake up ten bales of hay ever' day and milk sebem head of cows."

She went to work for the old woman, and she put up the hay ever' day and milked the sebem head of cattle. After a while the gal decided to go back home and told the woman to pay her her wages. The witch didn't pay her in money, but she set out some colored boxes and said, "Take your su'prize box whenever you're ready to go."

The little gal finished up her work and when she was about to start a little bird flew up in her winder and commenced to sing:

> Pee wee, take the blue;
> Pee wee, take the blue.

She took the blue box and started out. This box had the witch's gold and silver in it, and the witch took out atter her. The little gal saw her a-coming and run on till she come to the sheep. She said, "Sheep, sheep, hide me; the old witch's coming."

The sheep said, "All right, crawl up in my wool."

She crawled up in the sheep's wool and hid. And the old witch come up to the sheep and said, "Sheep o' mine, sheep o' mine, have you seen ary gal go up through here with my little blue box?"

The sheep said, "Yeaw, she went by here about an hour ago. You can't catch her."

The witch turned around and started back to the house. The little gal crawled out of the sheep's wool and started on. The witch saw her and took out atter her again. The little gal run on as fast as she could go and come to the cow. She said, "Cow, cow, hide me; I see the old witch a-coming."

The cow said, "All right, crawl up in my hoof."

The little gal crawled up in the cow's hoof, and in a minute the old witch come up and said, "Cow o' mine, cow o' mine, have you seen ary gal go up through here with my little blue box?"

The cow said, "Yeaw, she went up through here about an hour ago. You can't catch her."

The old woman looked about awhile and turned around and started back home. The little gal come out of the cow's hoof and started on. The old witch saw her and took atter her again. The little gal saw her a-coming and run on till she come to the apple tree.

Said, "Apple tree, apple tree, hide me; I see the old witch coming."

The apple tree said, "All right, climb up in my sprouts."

The little gal clomb up in the sprouts and hid. Soon the old woman come up to the tree and said, "Apple tree o' mine, apple tree o' mine, have you seen ary gal go up through here with my little blue box?"

The apple tree said, "Yeaw, she went up through here about an hour ago. You can't catch her."

The old witch looked around the apple tree and didn't see nothing, so she started home. The little gal come out of the tree and started on up the road. And the witch seen her and come on after her again. The little gal run on till she come to the log and said, "Log, log, hide me; I see the old witch a-coming."

The log said, "All right, crawl up in my holler then and she can't find ye." She crawled up in the log.

The old witch come along and said, "Log o' mine, log o' mine, have you seen ary gal go up through here with my little blue box?"

The log said, "Yeaw, she went up through here about an hour ago. You can't catch her."

The old witch went up to the end of the log and looked up in there, but the little gal stopped the holler up and it was so dark the old witch couldn't see nothing. So she went back home.

The little gal got out of the log and went on home. When she got there and didn't have nothing, her stepmother got mad at her and put her out in the hogpen to live. She washed up the hog pen and made her a clean place to live, and then she opened up her su'prize box and found it was full of gold and silver. She took it out and started counting it. The other ugly gal slipped around and saw her and went and told her mammy. The mother come out there and saw it and she said, "If you done that good, I'll send my gal off to work."

So she told her ugly gal to take off and hunt her a job of work. She went out there and jumped in the well. And she come to the log in the road and the log said, "Go around me, go around me, little gal."

But the ugly gal just stepped on the log and went on. She come to the apple tree and started to climb it and get some apples. The apple tree said, "Get all the apples you want, but don't break my sprouts."

Well, she clomb around in the tree and broke ever' sprout offen it. She went on and come to the cow and started milking it. The cow said, "Get all the milk you want and hang the bucket back on my horns."

But she drunk all the milk she wanted and throwed the bucket on the ground. Went on till she come to the sheep. She started shearing the sheep. The sheep said, "Get all the wool you want and hang the shears back on my horns."

But she took all the wool the sheep had and throwed the shears on the ground. She went on till she come to the house, and she hollered and told the woman she wanted a job of work. The witch said, "You can work here, but you have to put up ten bales of hay and milk by sebem cows ever' day."

The ugly gal started working, but she never ruck up enough hay and she never milked all the cows. The old witch never could get her to do up all the work. And when the time come for her to go home, she asked for her pay, and the old witch set out a lot of purty boxes and said, "You can take your su'prize box whenever you're ready, and I'm going to whup you all the way home."

The little ugly gal got ready to go and a little bird flew up in her winder and said:

> Pee wee, take the red;
> Pee wee, take the red.

The ugly gal come out and took the red box and lit out for home. She looked back and saw the old witch coming with a big long switch. She run till she come to the sheep and bagged it to hide her, but the sheep said, "I can't, my wool is too short." She come to the cow and bagged it to hide her, but the cow said, "I can't, my sack is empty and I have to pick grass." She come to the apple tree and bagged it to hide her, but the apple tree said, "I can't, I hain't got no sprouts." About that time the witch come up to her. She run on to the log and bagged it to hide her, but the log said, "I can't, my holler is stopped up." The old witch give her two big licks with that switch, and she jumped over the log and run to the well.

She come up the well and went home, and her mother grabbed that red su'prize box and opened it up. And out of the box come rattlesnakes and copperheads and eat the mother and the little ugly gal up.

That purty gal lived there happy ever after.

The next story, principally about Jack and his bull, was so rare and so closely related to the girls with one, two, and three eyes that the indexers of European tales did not give it a separate number, but attached it to Type 511 with an asterisk. This version still has a recognizable skeleton of Type 511. Jim, the teller, said about it: "That's the way my mother allas related that tale to us ever since I was just a little shaver. I guess she repeated that un more than any other. Hit was my favor-ite and I've allas liked to tell it." It is No. 6 in the microcard edition.

JACK AND THE BULL STRAP

Once there was a married man and he had one son, and his wife died, and he married again. And his second wife had three daughters and didn't like his son Jack. So she took a notion she would starve him to death. His father would come in, and Jack would be a-setting out behind the house on a rock. He'd be a-crying, and his father would say, "What's the matter, Jack?"

He said, "I'm a-starving to death."

His wife would say, "Look at his little old greasy mouth!" Said, "He's been eating and stuffing all day."

His father said, "Well, I guess you've had enough today, Jack."

The second time when the father was about to come home, the stepmother caught him and greased his mouth and made it appear like he'd been a-eating. His father come in and found him out on that rock a-crying. He said, "What's the matter, son?"

He said, "I'm a-starving to death."

She said, "Hit's not so," said, "look at his little old greasy mouth. He's been eating and stuffing around all day."

The next day he was out on his rock setting and crying, and his little bull come along, said, "What's the matter, Jack?"

He said, "I'm a-starving to death."

He said, "You knock off one of my horns and eat." Said, "If you don't get enough out of it, you knock off the other'n and help yourself. They's plenty more in it."

Jack knocked the horn off the bull's head, and he eat all he wanted. Put it back on. The bull said, "Now when you get hungry, you get out here and whistle, and I'll come."

The next day Jack he was setting out whistling on his rock. The little bull come up, and he eat. He played and run around the house. The stepmother noticed him, said, "Well, Jack," said, "What're you living on?"

He said, "I'm a-living on the fat of my guts, what'd ye think?"

She said, "I know that ain't so." Said, "Tomorrow I'll send old One Eye out to watch ye."

Well, the next day he went out, and she sunt old One Eye out. He whistled and whistled, and finally he whistled old One Eye to sleep. Up come his little bull, and he eat. Old One Eye went back in the house, and his stepmother said, "Well, what did he live on, One Eye?"

She said, "Law me, mother," said, "I couldn't tell." Said, "He whistled the purtiest whistling I ever heared and whistled me to sleep."

She said, "I'll know tomor'. I send old Two Eyes."

Next day she sunt old Two Eyes to watch him. Jack set on his rock, and he whistled and he whistled and he whistled old Two Eyes to sleep. Up come his little bull, and he eat. She went back to the house. "What did he live on, Two Eyes?"

"Law me, mother," said, "I couldn't tell. He whistled the purtiest whistling I ever heared and whistled me to sleep."

She said, "I'll know tomor'." Said, "I'll send old Three Eyes."

The next day she sunt old Three Eyes. And Jack set down on his rock, and he whistled and he whistled. He whistled two of her eyes asleep and the other'n almost shot. Up come his little bull, and he took off a horn and he eat. Well, old Three Eyes went back to the house, and the old woman asked her, "What did he live on, old Three Eyes?"

She told her, "He eat all he wanted out of one horn of his little bull."

Well, this old lady took a notion to fool him, and so she got down sick. Jack asked her, "What's the matter?"

She said, "Oh, it wouldn't do no good to tell you."

He said, "It might," said, "tell me what it is ails ye."

She said, "I'm a-longing for your bull's heart."

Jack knowed what the matter was, but he never let on. He says, "All right," says, "you make me up the last of the wheat dough to cap over his eyes and hold him for me, and I'll knock him in the head, and you shall have his heart."

Well, she fixed up her wheat dough and took it to Jack. He
caught his little bull and had her hold it, and he took the dough
and he capped them wheat plasters over *her* eyes and knocked
her in the head.

He jumped on his bull and took off. He rode till dark and
decided to spend the night by the edge of the woods. Jack
he clomb a tree, and his little bull slept at the roots. They got
up the next morning, and the little bull said to Jack, said, "Jack,
I had an awful dream last night."

Jack asked him, "What did ye dream?"

The bull said,

> "I dreamed that me and a bear fit and fit;
> It almost killed me, but I killed it.

But if it kills me, you take three raw straps out of my back,
and whoever asks your name, tell 'em Jack and the Bull Strap."

Well, Jack said he would, and he got on his bull's back and
he rode on till about ten o'clock and he looked out and he
saw the bear a-coming. He got off of his bull and clomb a tree.

> The bull and the bear fit and fought and fit;
> The bear almost killed the bull, but the bull killed it.

Jack got down, and he rode his bull on till dark overtuck
him again. He clomb a tree, and his bull slept at the roots.
Well, the next morning when he clomb down, the bull said,
"Jack, I had a worser dream than ever last night."

He said, "What did you dream?"

It said,

> "I dreamt that me and a lion fit and fit and fit;
> It almost killed me, but at last I killed it.

But if it kills me, you do this. You take three raw straps out
of my back, and whoever asks your name, you tell them Jack
and the Bull Strap."

They went on till it got up in the day, and Jack looked out
and saw the lion a-coming. He jumped off and clomb a tree.

> They fought and fit and fought and fit;
> The lion almost killed the bull, but the bull killed it.

They rode on till dark overtaken them again. Jack he clomb a tree, and the bull he slept at the roots. The next morning the bull said, "Jack," said, "I had a *nawful* dream last night."

Jack said, "Why, what did you dream last night?"

Said,

> "I dreamt that me and a pant'er fit and fit and fit;
> I almost killed the pant'er, but it killed me.

And if it kills me, Jack, you take three raw straps out of my back, and whoever asks your name, tell 'em Jack and the Bull Strap."

They went on till about ten o'clock, and Jack looked off and he saw the pant'er a-coming. Jack jumped off his bull's back and clomb a tree. And they fit and they fit. The bull almost killed the pant'er, but the pant'er killed the bull. Jack he got down and he cut him three raw straps out of the bull's back and went on.

He went on and on, and he met a man driving a wagon. He said, "What's your name, son?"

He said, "Jack and the Bull Strap."

Said, "If you don't tell me better than that," said, "I'll cut you in two with this ox whip."

"Tie him down," said Jack, "And wring his head twicet around."

The strap come from around his middle and started wringing the man's head off.

He said, "Spare my life, Jack, and I'll give you my wagon and team."

Jack put his straps away, took his wagon and team on off, and went on till he come to a king's house. He hired to herd the king's sheep. The king said, "Well, Jack," said, "they are an old two-headed giant lives down there." Said, "He kills ever'-body I hire to herd sheep."

Jack said, "He won't kill me."

"Yes, he will; you're the smallest feller I ever hired to do it."

He hired Jack just the same and sunt him over there. Jack was herding the sheep around, and up the road come the old giant with two heads. He said, "What're you a-doing here?"

Jack said, "Letting my sheep eat grass."

He said, "Get outten here; I'll kill you and your sheep, too."

"Tie him down," said Jack, "and wring one of his heads off and the other'n twicet around."

The old giant said, "Spare my life, Jack, and I'll give you a hoss, bridle, saddle, and a fine suit of clothes."

Jack said, "Deliver 'em up here, sir!"

He took up his straps and collected his rewards from the old giant and went on off. Got a job working for another king. Hired out to herd sheep again. The old king said, "They're an old three-headed giant lives down there. He'll kill you. He kills ever' man I get to herd sheep."

Jack said, "He won't kill me."

King said, "Yes, he will; you're no bigger than the others."

He hired Jack to herd his sheep. Jack went down to the place and was herding sheep all right, and the old giant rode up. Said, "What're you a-doing here?"

He said, "I'm a-letting my sheep eat grass."

He said, "If you don't get out of here I'll kill you and your sheep too."

"Tie him down," said Jack, "And wring two of his heads off and the other'n twicet around."

"Spare my life, Jack, and I'll give you a hoss, bridle, saddle, and a fine suit of clothes."

Jack said, "Deliver 'em up here, sir!"

He took his goods and he went on to another old king's house. Hired to herd sheep with him. The old king said, "They're a four-headed giant lives down yander. He kills ever' man I hire to herd my sheep."

Jack said, "He won't kill me."

King said, "Yes, he will; you're a runtier man than the others."

Jack was a-herding his sheep, and the old giant rode up. Said, "What're you a-doing here?"

"Letting my sheep eat grass."

"Get out of here; I'll kill you and your sheep too."

"Tie him down," said Jack, "and wring three of his heads off and the other'n twicet around."

"Spare my life, Jack, and I'll give you a hoss, bridle, saddle, and a fine suit of clothes."

Jack said, "Deliver 'em up here, sir!"

Jack got his goods, took up his bull straps, and rode on. He went to another old king's house and fell in love with the king's daughter. They's about to get married, and this old king didn't approve of it. He set a day to kill his girl by drownding her. She was out crying. Jack rode up, said, "What's the matter?"

"Won't do me any good to tell ye."

"Yes, it will."

She said, "They've set a day to drownd me."

Jack said, "No, they won't," said, "I've got horses that'll beat far and squirt water into the briny ocean."

The day come that he had set to drown her, and they put her out and the water was all up around her. Jack run in with his horses, beat the far and squirted the water into the briny ocean. They didn't get to drownd her.

Well, the next day she was out a-crying again, and Jack rode up, said, "What's the matter?"

She said, "They've set a day to burn me."

Jack said, "No, they won't."

She said, "Yes, they will."

He said, "No, they won't." Said, "I've got horses that'll beat the far and squirt water into the briny ocean."

Well, when the day come they'd set to burn her, she was out and the far was roaring up all around her. And Jack rode in with his horses. He beat the far and squirted water into the briny ocean.

He took the king's daughter up behind him and rode off with her. They's married and lived happy thereafter.

Joe Couch contributed two or three excellent *Märchen* to the collection after the other boys had talked out. He had some trouble recalling all the episodes of the magic deer story and was helped out by his wife and small son. He had heard it back in the dim past, and when he was through reciting it, Jim spoke up and said that he had heard it from an Aunt Shepherd. It is mostly Type 303, one of the rarest types to be found in America. It is No. 57 in the microcard edition.

THE MAGIC WHITE DEER

Once there was a couple of twin boys that favored—you couldn't tell one from the other they was so exactly alike. In their growing up, one of them had cut off his big toe, maybe with an ax. He had a toe off of one foot, and that was the only way you could tell them apart.

They took a notion to set out and seek their fortune one day, and traveled and traveled along the road a long ways, until they come to the forks of the road where it split and went different ways. One of them said, "All right, brother, we are going to part here. We will stick this knife right here in the forks of the road in the grass." And he said, "You go your journey, and if you happen to come back here and this knife is rusty, it'll mean I'm in danger. You foller my direction and try to trace me down, and I'll do the same—so if something happens to either one of us, the other can locate him."

The boys separated and went on their ways. One of the boys traveled till he come into a section of the country where there was a white deer that was going through killing all the young girls and carrying them away. He came up and stayed all night with a rich farmer who had an awful good looking girl. They was worrying about their girl, keeping her in and scared for her to get out where the white deer could find her and carry her off. She and the boy got to talking and soon were good friends, and he worried about it too, and he said, "I think I'll get out and hunt it." Soon it passed through, and he got a

glimpse of it, and he said, "I believe I can kill it. Believe I can track it down."

Her daddy said, "If you'll kill it, you can have my daughter." He said, "You can get my dogs—they's about five big hounds here—and get my rifle-gun and I'll furnish you with ammunition."

Well, he started hunting after it. He got in sight of it once and the dogs were close on it. They run it up a big oak tree in a certain place on the mountain. Well, he come up under the tree and he could hear it up there shivering like it was freezing. He hollered and told it to come down and he shot at it, but it would shiver again and tremble like it was freezing. He said, "I'm freezing."

Twin said, "Well, come on down."

And he said, "No, I'm afraid of your dogs."

The twin said, "My dogs won't hurt you."

The deer said, "I'll drop a stick down, and you tetch the dogs, and then I'll come down."

And so he dropped a stick down, a little twig or branch from the tree, and the twin picked it up and tetched one of his dogs with it, and it turned to a rock. When he tetched 'em all, they every one turned into rocks. When he dropped the stick at his feet, he turned into a rock too. And that was the end of them. The white deer come down and went on where it was going.

His brother made his journey out into the land and finally come back to the forks of the road where they parted. He went to the knife, and it was rusty, the blade was. He said, "Well, something is wrong with my brother." He started down his fork of the road tracing him.

He come up to this farmer where his brother had been. When he come in, they thought it was the same one and they wanted to know about his hunt, "Where have you been, where are your dogs and gun?" He saw that they talked strange and he just shook his head and wouldn't talk much. They worried over him and thought his mind had changed. But that night he pulled off his shoes and his toe was gone, they knowed this was another boy and mentioned it to him. He told them about his lost twin brother and how they had set out on different roads to seek their fortunes. They told him about this white deer raging through the country, and said, "Your brother follered it and he has never returned." He told them he knowed his brother was in trouble, and they said, "It passed through here and he got a glimpse of it."

The twin said, "I believe I can capture it if you'll furnish me the equipment I want." The man said he would furnish him with everything. He said, "Run me three silver bullets and put 'em in with the lead balls for my gun, and give me five dogs, and I'll trace it down."

He started with his dogs and gun, and chased it on and on till he come to its main hideout in the forest, up that big old oak tree. The boy walked under the tree and could tell it was up in there by the way the tree trembled, and the deer whined like it was freezing. He said, "Come on down."

It said, "No, I'm afraid of your dogs," said, "I'll drop this stick down, and if you'll touch your dogs—" Before it could finish talking, the boy had loaded his gun with a lead ball and he cracked down at it. It just shivered and said, "Uuh, I'm a-freezing."

He said, "Well, maybe this will warm you up a little." He put a silver bullet and cracked down and shot the deer through the shoulder. He fell down a distance and lodged, and when he lodged, he was taking on and saying, "I'm freezing; don't kill me."

"Well," the boy said, "tell me where my brother and his animals are."

The deer said, "If you promise you won't kill me, I'll drop this stick down, and you tetch certain rocks there you see." He dropped the stick down, and when the twin tetched a rock, it turned into a dog. He tetched another and another and turned all of the rocks back into dogs. And when he come to the last one and tetched it, his brother rose up before him. They fell on one another's necks when they found they were alive and well again. And this second twin said, "You can have that rich farmer's daughter if you take back this deer. Here is the magic stick. You tetch it when I make it come on down with this silver bullet."

When he pointed the gun at it, the deer promised to come down. When it landed on the ground, the first twin touched it, and it turned into the purtiest gal they had ever seen. And the first twin said, "Since I have a purty girl myself and you saved my life, I'll give this one that has been enchanted to you."

They come on in to the home of the rich farmer, and both married and settled down in that section and lived happy ever after.

The only folktale that the old man Tom knew was about the three girls seeking their fortune. Although he knew it well, I did not take it on the recorder at his cabin, but had Jim to tell it for this study. It belongs with ordinary folktales, Type 328; it is the European version of the British Jack and the Bean Stalk and is No. 8 in the microcard edition. Both the tellers called it

POLLY, NANCY, AND MUNCIMEG

Once upon a time there was an old widder-woman, and she had three daughters. One was named Polly, one was named Nancy, and one was named Muncimeg. The old lady taken sick, and she divided up her inheritance. She give Polly the house and garden, she give Nancy the rest of the land, and she give Muncimeg her old pocket penknife and her gold ring. Muncimeg thought she was cheated and she said, "Law me, mommy, you just give me this old pocket penknife and gold ring."

The mother said, "You keep 'em, and they'll come in handy when you are in trouble." And she died.

Well, they made it up to go on a journey to seek their fortune, Polly and Nancy did. And Polly said, "Well, what will we do with Muncimeg?"

Nancy said, "We'll lock her up in the house."

They locked her up in the house and started on their journey. After they got down the road a piece, Muncimeg started to worrying and taking on about her fortune. She said, "Law me, my mommy's old pocket penknife and gold ring." The door flew open, and she had nothing to do but take out after 'em.

Polly looked back and said, "Law me, sister Nancy, I see sister Muncimeg a-coming." Said, "What will we do with her?"

Nancy said, "Le's kill her!"

"No," said Polly, "le's take her with us."

"No, le's not," said Nancy; "le's stop her up here in this old holler log."

They put her in the holler log, stopped her up good, and went on. Muncimeg was crying and taking on.

She didn't let them get far along till she said, "Law me, my mommy's old pocket penknife and gold ring." The stopping come out of that old log. Out she come and after 'em she went again.

Polly heared her coming and stopped and said, "Law me, sister Nancy, I see sister Muncimeg a-coming again." Said, "What will we do with her this time?"

"Le's kill her."

"No, le's let her go with us."

"No, le's stop and put her here in this old holler tree."

Well, they stopped her up in the old holler tree and went on. Muncimeg let 'em get gone and she said, "Law me, my mommy's old pocket penknife and gold ring." Out come the stopping, and out she come and away she went after them.

Nancy heared her behind 'em and said, "Law me, sister Polly, I see sister Muncimeg a-coming. What will we do with her?"

"Le's kill her."

"No, le's let her go with us."

Well, they agreed to let her go along with them. They went along till they come to an old giant's house, and they stopped to stay all night. The old giant had three girls, and they put these three girls in a room to sleep with his three girls. The old giant was up 'way in the night whetting his knife, and Muncimeg, who had stayed awake, raised up and asked him, says, "What are you whetting that knife for?"

"Aah, go to sleep. Cut meat in the morning."

He whetted right on on his knife and then went to his old lady and asked her, "How can I tell our three girls from them three girls?"

The giant's old lady said, "Why, our three girls wears nightcaps."

Well, old Muncimeg heared 'em talking, and she eased up and slipped the nightcaps off the giant's girls' heads and put 'em on her head and her two sisters' heads. The old giant come in, and he cut his three girls's heads off in place of the others'. Old Muncimeg knowed all about it of course, and early next morning she waked Polly and Nancy and helped 'em escape before the giant and his wife waked up.

They wandered along the road that day and come to the king's house. He put 'em up for the night, and while they's a-talking, the old king told them about the old giant living across the way a piece. He told them he had three sons and said, "I'll give you my oldest son for the oldest if one of you will go to that old giant's house and drownd his old lady."

Well, the next morning they talked around and bagged Muncimeg into taking him up on it. She went to the old giant's house and laywayed the well. When the old lady come out to draw water, she headed her in the well—drownded her—and the old giant heared the racket and come running out there. Saw who it was and took after Muncimeg just a-roaring, "I'm going to pay you for this, Muncimeg. You caused me to kill my three girls and now you've drownded my old woman. I'm going to pay you for this!"

Muncimeg come to the river and couldn't make it across.

She said, "Law me, my mommy's old pocket penknife and gold ring." And she leaped the river and went back to the king's house. The king give her his oldest son to her oldest sister Polly.

"Well," he said, "I'll give you my next oldest for your other sister if you'll steal his horse, and the horse the giant has is covered with gold bells."

Muncimeg agreed to go back again and steal his horse. She got him out of the barn and she started riding him, and them bells started rattling. The old giant he woke up and jumped out of bed and run out there after her.

Muncimeg saw him a-coming and said, "Law me, my mommy's old pocket penknife and gold ring." And she become small and jumped into the horse's year and hid. Well, the giant tuck the horse and put him back in the barn, went back to sleep. She come outten his year and started riding him off again. The bells started rattling. The old giant heared 'em and he jumped out to see about his horse.

Muncimeg heared him and she said, "Law me, my mommy's old pocket penknife and gold ring." And she become small and jumped under his mane and hid. Giant tuck him and put him back in the barn and went back and got in bed and went to sleep. Muncimeg come out from his mane and started off. The giant took after her, but she was too far gone. He called out, "Hey, Muncimeg, I'll pay you for this. You caused me to kill my three girls, you drownded my old woman, and now you've stold my horse. I told you I'd pay you for this!"

Muncimeg come to the river with the old giant right behind her. She said, "Law me, my mommy's old pocket penknife and gold ring." And the horse jumped the river with her, and she rode in to the king's house.

The king was glad to see her come in with it and give her his next oldest son for her older sister Nancy. He said, "Now I'll give you my youngest son for yourself if you'll steal his gold. He sleeps with it under his head."

Muncimeg went back over there, found the gold sack under

the old giant's head, and while he was asleep, she slipped it out and started to run away from there. She slipped and fell, and the old giant come up from there and caught her. He took her in the house and tied her up in a sack and hung her up to the joist. He said, "I told you, Muncimeg, I'd pay you for this. You caused me to kill my three girls, you drowned my old woman, you stold my horse, and now you're trying to steal my gold. I told you I'd pay you for it. I'm going to make you mew like a cat, bew like a dog, and I'm going to make your old bones ring like teacups and saucers, knives and forks."

He went out to get him a frail to frail her with. She said, "Law me, my mommy's old pocket penknife and gold ring," and down come the sack and out she come. She caught his old dog and cat and put 'em in the sack and rounded up all his knives and forks, teacups and saucers. Put 'em all in the sack and hung it back up to the joist. She got outside the house and listened for him.

The old giant come back with a big frail, and the first lick he warped the sack, "Mew" went his cat. The next lick he warped, "Bew" went his dog. The next lick he warped it, he broke up his dishes and teacups and saucers. "I told you, Muncimeg, I'd pay you for it!"

When he tuck the sack down, he poured out his old cat and his old dog and all of his broke-up dishes. And he looked out and saw Muncimeg making it for the river. He tuck out after her, calling, "I told you so, Muncimeg, I'd make you pay for this. You caused me to kill my three girls, you drowned my old woman, stold my horse, stold my gold, you caused me to kill my dog and cat and caused me to break all my dishes. I told you I'd pay you for it!"

He was gaining on her by the time she got to the river. She said, "Law me, my mommy's old pocket penknife and gold ring," and over the river she went, safe from the old giant. She took the gold back to the old king's house, she got the king's youngest son for a husband, and they all went back home and lived happy.

Simple animal tales are very rare among the American white population. I had collected only two or three different types until I came to the Couch family, where, fortunately, several interesting Old World tales were still told. Most of these were in the repertory of Dave, and one of his most delightful tales is about the fox and the cat on a journey, Type 20. It is No. 32 in the microcard edition.

THE FOX AND THE CAT

Once there was a fox started out of the woods to hunt him something to eat, and he went along the road and met a cat. The cat said to the fox, "Where you going?"

"To seek my fortune."

"May I go too?"

"Yeaw, company's good sometimes."

The fox and the cat then went on and on till they met a hen. The hen said, "Where are you goin'?"

"We're going to seek our fortune."

"May I go too?"

"Company's good sometimes."

The three of 'em went on and on till they met a duck. The duck said, "Where are you going?"

"To seek our fortune."

"May I go too?"

"Yeaw, company's good sometimes."

All the animals went on and on till they met a drake.

"Where are you goin'?"

"To seek our fortune."

"May I go too?"

"Yeaw, company's good sometimes."

All the animals went on and on till they met a goose. Goose said, "Where are you goin'?"

"To seek our fortune."

"May I go too?"

"Yeaw, company's good sometimes."

Took the old goose along and went on till they met an old gander. Gander said, "Where are you all goin'?"

"Goin' to seek our fortune."

"May I go too?"

"Company's good sometimes."

They all went along the road till they met a turkey. Turkey said, "Where are you goin'?"

"To seek our fortune."

"May I go too?"

"Yeaw, company's good sometimes."

They went on and on till they met an old gobbler. Gobbler said, "Where're you all goin'?"

"Goin' to seek our fortune."

"May I go too?"

"Yeaw, company's good sometimes."

Well, the fox thought they was ready to travel by now, and so he led the whole gang along the road and off into the fields. Purty soon it was up in the day, and they all commenced to get hungry, and the fox started studying how he was goin' to get to eat one of them travelers. Finally they come to a log, and the fox said, "Well, le's all set down on this log and tell our fortunes. I'll give your names, and which one has the ugliest name will have to die." They all agreed and set down in a row on the log. The old fox began:

"Foxy Loxy purty name, Catty Latty purty name, Henny Penny purty name, Ducky Lucky purty name, Drakey Lakey purty name, Goosey Loosey purty name, Gander Lander purty name, Turkey Lurkey purty name, Gobbler Lobbler—ugly name."

They all jumped on the old gobbler and eat him up.

They traveled on through the evening and made camp in a tree that night. Went on the next day till they begin to get hungry again. Come to a log and they set down on it to hear their fortune again. The fox said:

"Foxy Loxy purty name, Catty Latty purty name, Henny Penny purty name, Ducky Lucky purty name, Drakey Lakey purty name, Goosey Loosey purty name, Gander Lander purty name, Turkey Lurkey—ugly name." So they jumped on the old turkey and made a meal out of her.

They got goin' again and traveled on and traveled on. Stayed in a tree that night and went on till up in the day. Commenced getting hungry again. The fox said, "Here's another log. Le's set down and hear your fortune again." They set down and he started out:

"Foxy Loxy purty name, Catty Latty purty name, Henny Penny purty name, Ducky Lucky purty name, Drakey Lakey purty name, Goosey Loosey purty name, Gander Lander—ugly name." So they made a meal out of the old gander that day.

Went on till the next day and come to a log, set down to hear the fox tell their fortune. He started out:

"Foxy Loxy purty name, Catty Latty purty name, Henny Penny purty name, Ducky Lucky purty name, Drakey Lakey purty name, Goosey Loosey—ugly name." So they made their meal offen the old goose.

Went on and stayed all night and traveled till up in the day. They come to a log and set down to hear their fortune again. The fox started out:

"Foxy Loxy purty name, Catty Latty purty name, Henny Penny purty name, Ducky Lucky purty name, Drakey Lakey —ugly name." And so they eat up the old drake.

Well, they went on till it come night. Stayed in the woods and traveled till up in the day. When they begin to get hungry, again the fox stopped 'em on a log and started:

"Foxy Loxy purty name, Catty Latty purty name, Henny Penny purty name, Ducky Lucky—ugly name." And they eat up the old duck.

Went on, and when the next day come and they was hungry, the fox stopped at a log and started telling fortunes:

"Foxy Loxy purty name, Catty Latty purty name, Henny Penny—ugly name." The fox and the cat eat up the old hen.

So the fox and the cat went on and on. Got along good together that night and traveled till way up in the day. Finally

they come to a log and they climbed it, and the fox started
telling the cat's fortune:

"Foxy Loxy purty name, Catty Latty ugly—"

Cat jumped off the log and started telling the old fox's
fortune:

"Catty Latty, purty name, Foxy Loxy ugly name—"

Fox said, "Foxy Loxy purty name, Catty Latty ugly name—"

They fell into a quarrel about which one had the ugliest
name, and they fit and they fought and they fit, and finally they
eat each other up. The fox eat the cat and the cat eat the fox.
And that was the fortune of all them animals.

A good proportion of mountain story and legend is made up
of witch and ghost material that has more traditional currency
than the local witchcraft. Dave told the following scare story,
making it so weird that Jim poked his head in from another
room and said, "Gosh, you're making that thing sound awful
lonesome." This version has some relation to Type 366 and
has been a favorite apparently in the South. It is No. 33 in the
microcard edition.

TAILIPOE

I'll tell you a tale now about an old lady who lived by herself
near the forest. She had two dogs, and the name of one was
old You Know and the other was named I Know. Something
got to bothering her and prowling around her log house. She
had a nawful bad door, made of old boards, and she was always
afraid something would get in at her oldtime door. Of a cold
night this strange varmint would get to freezing, and it would
try the house, and go around and around it, and stop and try
that door.

One night when it was prowling around the house, it stopped
at the door and worked around it and at the crack till it stuck
its old big tail under the door. It was about sixteen feet long,

I've allas heared, and she grabbed her ax and cut that old thing's tail off. Well, after she cut its tail off, she set them dogs on that thing and they run it away down in the big timber woods, eight or ten miles down in the valley below her house. Them dogs treed that thing down there and barked and barked till they got tard. And they come back to the house. Soon as they got back, they heared that thing coming up in the valley moaning and crying. It was saying, "You Know and I Know, all I want is my taaaaail-iiiii-poooooooe!"

And they tell me that to this day down in them big timber woods where the dogs treed that animal, the wind blows through the trees and they can hear a moaning voice, saying, "YouuuUUU KnoooOOOOOOOOOOoow, and I――KnoooO-OOOOOOoow, allll I――waaaaAAAAant isss myyyYYYYyyy taaaaaaaaAAAAAAAaail―iiiiii――poOOOOOe."

While we were discussing ghost tales one night, Jim gave a vivid account of such sessions at home when he was a boy. He said, "My mother would tell a scary tale along late bedtime, and me and my brother sleeping together in the back room would be afeared to leave the firelight. She would have to go to the room with us and hold the lamp till we got in the bed—and under the covers." He then told the following witch tale, one that is found in worldwide tradition, but was not given a type number. It is No. 29 in the microcard edition.

BRIDLING THE WITCH

Once they was two young men working at a place. One of them he got to looking awful thin and bad. The other'n asked him what was wrong with him. He told his buddy, he said, "If you went through of a night what I did," said, "you'd look bad too."

The other guy said, "Let me sleep in front tonight and see if it will happen to me."

Well, he laid in front that night. It got up along in the night, when in come a woman. Stood up over him, said a little ceremony she used. Had a little bridle in her hand, and when she was done, she popped that bridle on him and turned him into a horse. Took him out, riding him around. Went to an old place where they's having a big time, fiddling and dancing. Hitched him up and went in.

He went to trying to slip the bridle off of him. He'd rub and get it about off, and she'd know about it and run back out there and put it on and hook him back up to the fence. He kept on rubbing, and finally he got the bridle off. And after he got the bridle off, he turned back into his natural self again. He just grabbed the bridle and went in there where she's at and said the same words over her that she said over him and popped the bridle on her, jumped on her, and rode her.

He rode her to a blacksmith's shop and had her shod, and he rode her then to her husband's house. Told him he wanted to trade horses with him. They agreed to trade. He said, "Now, this filly's kindly skittish. You'll haft to lead her inside the barn before you take the bridle off of her."

He saddled this other horse and rode it off. This old guy he led the filly back into the barn and pulled the bridle off of her, and there stood his wife with horse shoes on her hands. He took his gun and shot her brains out. And that was the last of the witch.

The Couch material has a generous number of tall tales and Irishman anecdotes. The story of the one-eyed giant belongs to the tall type, having the giant episode followed by many pioneering exploits, such as those attributed to Daniel Boone and David Crockett. Although all three of the Couch men (Dave, Jim, and Joe) told slightly varying tales of Polyphemus, I chose Jim's to include here. These versions among the Couches are the only instances of the one-eyed giant in America that I know of. Judging from the episodes in the three versions, I feel that the source is the *Arabian Nights,* but it must have been learned by our ancestors in the Old Country. This mountain story has drawn into itself all of these types: 38, 1137, 1892, 1894, 1895, 1900. It is No. 7 in the microcard edition. All three tellers called it

THE ONE-EYED GIANT

Back in 1901 I was down in Mississippi, at Camp Shelby. I had me two companions down there, and we took a notion we would go on a fishin' trip down the Mississippi River. It was an awful wilderness down there where we went, and time we got down to where we wanted to go, we was lost. We looked away acrost the river and saw a little blue smoke boiling up out of a little shack. We got to callin' and hollerin' for help. Well, we called and called, and after while they was an old one-eyed giant— lived over there—after while he got his boat and come over and got us.

He took us over to his shack or cave where he lived. Now on the trip down the river we three men had to climb trees to get away from the snakes of a night and other varmints, and I had skinned a place on my belly. Purty bad sore. The old giant took us in to his cave and welcomed us. He started feedin' and fatterin' us up mighty good. But it looked like he was fatterin'· us up like a farmer a-fatterin' his hogs. He was goin' to eat us.

Well, it come a time, one of my buddies was good and fat. The old giant come and took him out. We never heard a thing of him again. And in a few days he come and took the other'n out and left me alone in his cave. Next time he come back I asked him, said, "Why, where's my buddies?"

He laughed and said, "Hawr, hawr, hawr. You needn't mind your buddies." Said, "They make good steak," and said, "when that sore's cured on your belly, you'll make a good steak, too!"

Now he'd go out of a day and he'd herd his goats. He had an awful good herd of goats. And he'd come back in of a night

and herd his goats in the cave and then lay down out front and sleep. I knowed my time was short when I saw that sore on my belly healin' up purty good. I had a notion one day that I would ex-cape. But when he'd come in to the cave and get ready to sleep, he'd set a big rock up in the cave door, after he'd herd his goats in. And they weren't no way for me to ex-cape out through it.

He went to sleep one evenin' in the front of the cave, and I took my chance. They was a big bunch of arn a-layin' around there, like pokin' sticks for his far. They was kindly sharp on one end. I took and chunked the far and helt them arns in that far till they got good and red. You know, he was a one-eyed giant. His eye was right in the middle of his fore'ead. I het them arns good and hot, and I slipped up to him, and I rammed about four of them right down that big eye. He raised from there a-buttin' them walls and a-carryin' on. He got right in the entrance of the cave and he roared out, *"You won't get away with this!"*

I managed to stay out of his way till he hushed, and then he moved the rock from over the cave door. And he set right in it. Well, he had one old goat there he called his pet. I picked that very old goat because he was the biggest and got right up between that goat's lags, right under the bottom of his belly, and got a-hold of his wool. I tried to stampede that goat herd out of there, but he stopped 'em and let 'em out one at a time. They kept a-goin' out of the cave, and this very old particular goat that I was on—or under, I mean—come up to the old giant and stopped. That old giant rubbed him over. He said, "I knowed you'd never fail me." Said, "You're my pet and I love ye." Was I scared! But it happened that he didn't find me, and the old goat passed on through.

When all of them passed on through and got out, he knowed that I'd somehow ex-caped. When I got out from there, I made for the river, and he come out of there a-squallin'. And when I looked around and down the river, I saw seven big other

giants a-comin'. I made my getaway and got to the boat in the
river and hopped in it. I felt awful anxious by the time I hit
that water. And by the time they all got up there, why I was
two-thirds of the way acrost. Now there was some great big
high mountains standin' on that side of the river bank, clifts
there that weighed tons. Well, they grabbed one of them clifts
and throwed it at me. In the place of sinkin' me they just
shoved me on all the way acrost.

When I come out of that danger, I had an old hog rifle-gun,
but I just had one bullet. I took up the riverbank and had to
climb trees at night from the snakes and wild varmints. One
day about noon I was settin' on the bank of the river, and of
course I was lost. There come along a great big flock of wild
geese and flew up in a water birch right over where I was a-set-
tin' and lit on a limb. I managed and studied how I would get
that flock with one bullet. Well, I finally thought of a way to get
all them geese at one shot. I shot right up through the middle of
that limb and split it, and it clamped back and caught all them
geese's toes. I clomb up the tree, took my old galluses, and tied
all them geese together and tied myself to them. I thought I'd
jump off with 'em to the ground. But instid, them geese flew
off with me.

They flew on and on with me, and when they got to goin'
further than I wanted to go, I just ripped out my knife and cut
the old strings that I had tied to 'em and myself. That dropped
me, and the luck was I fell right down in an old holler snag.
I felt something under my feet and rubbin' against my britches
legs. Felt awful soft, but I couldn't find out for a while what it
was. I soon found out it was some cub bears. I heard a racket
all at once comin' down the holler of that tree, just rip, rip, rip.
I reached up with my hand—I couldn't see—and just happened
to clinch an old bear right by the tail. Well, I had that old rusty
Barlow knife with the blade about half broke off. I tuck that
knife and I commenced jobbin' that bear, and she tuck right
back up that holler tree and carried me out the top.

I clomb down and started on. I didn't have any bullets left in my old hog rifle-gun, but you know we always carried a wiper an' ramrod. As I was goin' along, I loaded my old rifle with powder and with that wiper. Purty soon I come upon one of these old Russian wild boars and a bear a-fightin'. I taken aim with that wiper and killed that bear. And then me and the boar had it around a few trees. I took around a little sugar maple, about six, eight inches at the stump, and that boar made a lunge at me and hit that tree. His tush went plumb through it and come out on the other side. I grabbed me up a rock and bradded that tush on the other side, and there I had that old boar too.

Well, I went on home for a horse to come and get my meat. When I started to go across an old field by the river, I got tangled up in some old sawbriers and down I come. I fell on a whole flock of pateridges and killed 'em. Gathered up my pateridges and went on till I come to the river. I had to wade it, and I was so dirty and ragged I just left on my huntin' shirt. I waded that river, and when I come out, I'd caught a whole shirttail full of fish. I just rolled up my shirt like a poke and took 'em on.

I moved on in home. Well, the old horse I had he was awful pore, and he had a purty sore back from a saddle scald. But I got that old horse ready and started back with him to get my bear and boar. Got over in the woods purty close to where my wild meat was at, and that old horse slidded up and fell and hurt hisself, and he wasn't able to carry no bear in. I just stripped him and turned him loose in the woods, live or die.

You know, in about fifteen years after that, I was back in that same place again a-huntin'. I saw a tree a-shake, shake, shakin' up toward the top of the mountains. I decided to investigate and see what it was. I went up there and saw what it was. A acorn had fallen in the horse's back and made a acorn tree. A big gang o' wild hogs was follerin' that old horse around, bitin' his heels, making him kick up and shake off them acorns for 'em.

Of many short traditional items always good for a laugh in the Couch family, none are more popular than Irishman jokes. Many of them turn upon a pun or some other old-fashioned situation. Generally they are told singly by men who like to sit and swap them for hours at a time. But I found Jim joining them together into a string of adventures, six to eight at a time. He said about this, "I never did like to tell just one short joke." These are Nos. 14 to 19 in the microcard edition.

ARSHMAN AND THE WATCH

Once they was two Arshmen. They come over from England to America and was a-traveling along the road. One was named Pat and the other was named Mike. Come to the forks of the road, and one took one fork of the road and the other'n took t'other. They had been advised by fellers who had been over here that they was awful big ticks and varmints over here, and if they found such a thing, they was supposed to kill it.

Well, old Pat come along and he found a watch laying in the road a feller had lost. Had a chain on it. He picked that old watch up and helt it to his year, and the watch went tick, tick. The old Arshman said, "Fat [Faith] o' me Jesus," he said, "this is a tick and I'll smash him up."

He laid it down on a rock and took another rock and he smashed the watch all to pieces. He went on down the road and he met the man that had lost the watch hunting for it. The man said, "Did you find ary watch along the road?"

He said, "No, but, fat o' me Jesus," said, "I found a big tick back up yander."

Said, "What did you do with it?"

He said, "I smash him up."

"Go show me where it was."

He went and showed him, and it was his watch. He give him a string and said, "Now next thing you find like that on the road," said, "you tie this string to it and put it in your bosom pocket."

Old Pat went along the road, come to a mudhole in the road, and he went to cross it and he saw a little old young turkle [turtle] about the size of a watch. He reached down and picked it up, tied it by the leg with his string, and stuck it in his bosom. Went on a mile or two, and old Mike and him run together again. Mike looked at him a minute, saw that string, said, "Pat, fat o' me Jesus," said, "what time is it?"

Old Pat pulled that little turkle out, kicking, and he looked at it awhile. "Fat o' me Jesus, I don't know," he said. Pulled it out and had that old turkle tied by the leg, "Must be twelve, scratching for thirteen."

FROG OR MOOSE?

They went on along the road; both of 'em was broke. They tried to manage a plan to get 'em some rum. While they was going along, they found a big frog by the road. Old Pat said, "Mike, I'll take this frog along and call him a moose." Said, "I'll go in that saloon down yander, and I'll bet that man a dollar again' a quart of rum this is a moose. And he'll bet it's a frog." Said, "And we'll leave it to the next man comes in." Said, "You be by the side of the door and step in and say it's a moose."

Well, they went down, and old Pat went in. He was holding that old frog by the leg. Directly he said, "Mister, what is this?"

He said, "Why, it's a frog."

"No," he said, "it's a moose."

"No, it's nothing but a frog."

"I know it's a moose. I bet you a dollar again' a quart of rum that this is a moose, and we'll leave it to the next man steps in."

The old bartender said, "Well, I'll bet with ye."

They made their bet, and in a few minutes in stepped old Mike. Pat said, "Say, pardner, what is this, a frog or a moose?"

He said, "Why, that's a moose!"

That old bartender couldn't do nothing but hand him over a quart of rum.

FROGS AND THE RUM

Pat and Mike took their quart of rum and went on down the road. They come to a creek and walked along it a piece. Soon they heared a big bullfrog calling across the water, "Rum, rum, rum!" One of them old Arshmen said, "Fat o' my Christ, Pat, there that man is wanting some rum." Said, "Give him a drink."

He went and poured some rum in the creek where that old bullfrog was a-hollering. Went on. Drunk it all but a little. Went along beside the stream, and one of these here little bull-frogs heared 'em a-coming and he jumped into the creek and went, "Jug, jug, jug." Old Mike said, "By fat and by Jesus, Pat, he's wanting jug and all." Pat just throwed the whole jug in the creek. And they went on.

THE MON A-COMING

They went on through the country till they got awful hungry. They come to some apple trees with purty good apples on them. Mike clomb over the orchard fence to get some, and old Pat he was a-watching. And about then the moon begin to raise. Pat said, "Hey, Mike, I see the mon a-coming!"

Old Mike jumped out of that tree and tore out of there, and right down through the field he went. Thought it was a man coming after him. Went on down through there as fast as he could split it and passed a pasture field where some men had been raking hay and left the old rake a-laying on the ground. He stepped on that old rake, and the handle of it flew up and hit him in the back. He let out a yell and run on till he give out. He stopped till Pat come up, and then called and asked him, said, "Is the mon still a-coming?"

He said, "Yeaw, it's still a-coming."

Old Mike said, "Fat o' my Jesus, I want to stay out of his way," said, "he already give me one good whop as I went."

PICKING MULBERRIES

They went on, stayed all night with a fambly, and set out the next day. Got hungry again, and come to some mulberry trees. They had some berries on 'em. Old Pat he clomb the tree to shake some mulberries off and left old Mike on the ground gathering them up and eating 'em. Cows had laid out under the trees, and they was a lot of tumblebugs rolling their loads outten there. And old Mike was a-eating ever'thing that looked black, tumblebugs and all. He hollered up at Pat and said, "Hey, Pat, fat o' my Jesus, has mullems got laggums?"

Old Pat said, "Why, no, they don't have no laggums."

He said, "Fat o' my Jesus, I've just eat my belly full of spradling bugs then."

I'VE GOT THE JOB

They went on for another day or two, trying to get 'em a job of work along at the houses. After a few days Pat got a job from an old farmer to cut up a piece of corn. Told him he would give him two dollars to cut corn and shock it. He turned around to Mike and said, "Mike," said, "I'll give you two dollars if you'll help me cut up this piece of corn."

Mike said, "All right, I want a job here too, but," said, "tell me what you're going to get out of it?"

He said, "By fat and by Christ," said, "I've got the job, hain't I?"

The remarks that Jim and Dave made about riddling in the home were justified in the recording sessions. We had a long session one night at Jim's house when ten to fifteen men and boys were present. I briefed the riddlers first and then simply passed around the mike. The session went on with breaks for three hours. Many of these riddles are worldwide in tradition, but others have never to my knowledge appeared before and are not found in Archer Taylor's *English Riddles from Oral Tradition*.

> As I went around my world of Wiglam Waglam,
> There I found old Tom Tiglam Taglam;
> I called old Hellum Bellum
> To take old Tom Tiglam Taglam
> Out of my world of Wiglam Waglam.

This one, given by Dave, is not in Taylor. The answer is that a man named his cornfield Wiglam Waglam, his old boar Tom Tiglam Taglam, and his dog Hellum Bellum. The boar got into the corn field, and he called the dog to chase it out.

> Love I set, love I stand,
> Love I hold in my right hand,
> Love I see in yonders tree,
> If you can onriddle that
> You can hang me.

Another of Dave's, this is called a neck riddle, a type that Taylor did not include in his collection. Answer: a woman had to make a riddle to free her lover, and she took her little dog named Love, cut it in pieces, and put them in the places named. The jailer could not answer it, and the man went free.

> I went through heely veely,
> I looked over, and there believie,
> Saw a colliver planting caniver,
> Called to my nighest neighbor,
> Lend me his euney cuney crow,
> Kill a colliver I'd give him the calliverow.

This one, riddled by Jim, is in no collection that I have examined. Some of the words are made up from others, and a few words may be Irish or Scottish names for implements. Answer: a man saw a deer, called for his neighbor to lend him a gun and get a piece of the meat.

Humpy bumpy on the wall,
Humpy bumpy got a fall;
Ten men, a thousand more,
Can't fix humpy bumpy back
Like it was before.

Told by Dave, this is an interesting variant of Humptey
Dumptey, and it is found in Taylor, No. 739. The answer is,
of course, an egg.

What is it lives in a barn, eats corn and hay, and can see out
of one end as good as it can out o' the other?

Told by Frank, Jim's oldest son, this one is in no collection
that I have seen. The answer is a blind mule.

You don't need no pencil to answer this one, but I bet some
of you boys can't answer it. If you saw an electric train and it
was going east and the wind was blowing north, which way
would the smoke be going?

This one was posed by Frank. Although most had not heard it,
they were sharp enough to answer almost in a body. Answer:
"An electric train don't have no smoke."

Some legends of pioneering linger on in the memory of the
Kentucky mountain folk. They are told as truth, even as
adventures of members of a family. The following two legends
as told by Dave did not happen to the Couches but are yarns
to illustrate courage and cowardice on our early frontier.

SEVEN DEAD INDIANS

Now I'll tell you a Indian story, and hit was a true story. When
our people taken this nation away from the Indians and come
in here, we was thin settled in this country. More Indians in
some places than they was American people.

They was an old woman she lived by herself, and she had sebem chillern. The Indians had killed her man, and she was trying to stay on and raise up her fambly. When she went out of an evening to get her wood in, she had to be on the lookout for Indians. All the people had to work in danger, and the menfolks allas stood guard watching for 'em while the others worked. Well, this old woman was getting her wood, and she seed nine Indians hiding and slipping around, and she heared 'em talking about coming in when it got dark. She rushed back quick and got her wood and got supper for her chillern. She got 'em all nine in bed and lulled 'em asleep so they wouldn't get scared. Then she planned out a way to fight them Indians. Well, she had a hatchet-ax, a tommy hatchet they called it. And she opened the door just about big enough for one man to scrouge in at a time, and she spiked that door open, just leaving it so's it'd open no furder than that crack.

Well, along about dusty dark they come to make the attack on her. One crowded in that crack at the door, and she hauled away and split its brains out with that hatchet-ax. She dragged that un back and pitched it back in the floor. It kept on, one come after another, scrouging in that door, and she kept swinging that tommy hatchet till she killed all nine of them, piled 'em all up in a pile together. That's the way the women used to have to fight for their chillern back then.

OLD INDIAN BINGE

Yes, Indians used to come in and out of here and keep the people scared to death all the time. They was an old runigade Indian—he was a mixed breed, wa'n't full-blooded Indian—used to get him a bunch of runigades and travel this country, robbing and stealing. He was called old Indian Binge. Went through here several trips. They'd start from Virginia and come down Cumberland here and cross Pine Mountain, and then go back across maybe to Norton, Appalachia, and in there.

He come through Big Stone one time, had six more Indians with him. And them Indians kidnapped 'em a woman apiece and led them away, took 'em towards Norton above Appalachia. But the leader, old Indian Binge, he claimed he protected the women and kept the others from violating and killing them. Well, they took them women right up a rough creek into the hills. Them women would tear off bits of their dresses and throw down for their men to foller.

Their men come in that evening and heared the alarm and was directed the way they went. The Indians got back in what was later called Binge Branch where Binge had 'em to camp for the night, said it was for delay so the white men could overtake 'em. The men come upon them in their camp. Old Binge hope the whites, and they killed all the other six Indians and got their women back. They let old Indian Binge go because he did seem to know what was happening and tried to protect the women—at least he didn't do no violence that time.

Well, a little later after that happening, old Binge was back in this country again, with two more Indians with him. And the people figured if he wa'n't going to do no meanness, he was coming back to hunt treasures that the Indians allas claimed was in here. Well, it was norrated that he was in here for a treasure hunt, and a bunch of men got back in the Shell Gap of Pine Mountain and laywayed 'em. The Indians come along there. And right in the saddle of the mountain was a blackgum tree, and old Binge clomb that blackgum to get some mistletoe. They farred away at the men on the ground and killed one. The other man with him, called the Runner, got away and ex-caped back to Virginia. They leveled down on Binge, and one shot went right square through his head. They said old Indian Binge reached in his pocket and tuck out a silver cup and put it over the bullet hole and catched his brains in it. He fell dead at the roots of that blackgum tree. That was about the last Indians that ever come into this country. Atter that, they left it all to the whites.

A final story that might be entered here to indicate the rich heritage of the Couch folktales is the story of the robber brothers. It is so rare that there is only one version known in European tale tradition and that in a far-off Finnish-Sweden list. The Types Index gives it No. 1525*. The asterisk means that it is too rare to enter among the traditional tale types. And yet it was known by two of the Couches, and I have found another text in the repertory of a Leslie County man, who had heard it in about 1910 from a man who lived in Magoffin County, Kentucky. The last episode is in tradition, having the Type No. 1653B. This is Jim's version, which he called

NIP, KINK, AND CURLY

They was three boys once by the names of Nip, Kink, and Curly. Their parents died off and left them, and they decided to housekeep and live on there together. Nip and Kink thought they was wise, and they thought Curly was a fool.

Well, they took a notion after so long to turn out to be outlaws and go stealing for a living. They got together and made it up one night to go and steal 'em a goose. And old Curly said, "Boys," says, "let me go with you."

They said, "No," said, "we don't want you; you're too dumb."

Now Curly had heard what they said and what they was up to, so he took out another way and beat them through the woods to where they was figuring on stealing the goose. He asked that old feller, "What'll you give me to mind your goose pen tonight?" Said, "I know of two fellers a-going to steal your geese."

He said, "I wouldn't know," said, "what's your price?"

He said, "A big fat goose."

"All right."

"Give me a pair of pincers and show me to your goose pen."

He give Curly a pair of pincers, and he went and crawled in the goose pen. Along in the night here come old Nip and Kink. Kink said, "I'll watch, and you go in and get one."

Nip he went and he rammed his hand into the goose pen, and old Curly pinched him with them pincers. He run back out. He says, "I can't get nary un," says, "that gander bites so hard." Says, "Suppose you get one."

He said, "All right, you watch and I'll try it."

He went and run his hand in to get him a goose, and old Curly he clinched him with the pincers. He come out of there, said, "That old gander bites so hard I can't get nary un." Said, "Le's call it off and go back home, huh?"

They called it off for that night and went on back home without nothing. Next morning about sunrise here come old Curly carrying his big fat goose under his arm. They called, "Hey, Curly, where did you get that fat goose?"

He said, "Eh, I stold him last night."

Well, they got together that day and made it up, says, "Tomor' we'll go steal us a mutton." Curly heared 'em and come around, said, "Well, shall I go with ye?"

They said, "Nope, you can't go."

Well, old Curly went on another way and come to the feller's house and said, "I know of two fellers is going to steal your sheep tonight." Said, "What'll you give me to mind your sheep pen?"

He said, "I wouldn't know; what's your price?"

He said, "A good fat mutton."

He said, "All right."

"Give me a maul and show me to your sheep pen."

Old Curly took the maul and swung it up in the sheep pen. Along in the night here come Nip and Kink. Nip said, "Kink, you watch, and I'll go in and get us one."

He says, "All right."

He went in, and old Curly he drew back with that maul and swung it and out he put him. Nip run back and said, "Kink, that old ram butts so hard I can't get nary un. Supposen you try it."

He said, "All right," said, "you watch and I'll try it."

He walked in the door and he got a-holt of him a sheep and he started toward the door with it, and old Curly he drawed back with that maul and he pounded him right in the setter and out he put him. He went back, "Well," said, "that old ram butted me so hard I can't get nary un." Said, "Le's just go back home."

They went back home, and the next morning old Curly he come leading a fat sheep in. They said, "Where did you get him at?"

"Ah, I stold him last night."

Well, they said, "Now tomor' night we'll go steal something that can't butt nor bite."

Curly said, "Shall I go with ye?"

They said, "Yeaw," said, "we'll take you along with us to-night." Said, "I know of a man that's got a big smokehouse full of meat." Said, "We'll go steal us a big load o' meat."

Well, they went to that man's smokehouse, and Curly watched while Nip and Kink went in and shouldered 'em up a big load of meat, and they got purt' near all of it. When they come out, they told Curly to get a few pieces and bring the door to. Curly went in and got a few pieces and just took the door off the hinges and come on after 'em, and away they went. When they saw Curly with the door, they asked him, said, "What are you doing with the door, Curly?"

Curly said, "You fellers took nearly all the meat, so I thought I'd bring the door too."

They got on their way home and they heard a racket, and it was some fellers a-coming. They was a pine tree there by the side of the road. One of 'em said, "What shall we do? We don't want anybody to see us on the road with a load of meat this time of night."

Curly said, "Le's climb this pine tree."

They clomb up the pine tree, and Curly said, "Take my door up." They took his door up and got in the top of the tree. Directly they come two old robbers along and they was tired and hungry. They set right down under that tree, rested, and then went to counting their loot that they robbed. One of them said, "I'm so hungry I could tie my belly in a knot."

The boys heared it, and Curly sliced off a nice piece of meat and pitched it down to 'em. He pitched it down right where they was at. One of 'em grabbed it and looked at it, said, "Glory be, some good old meat—come down from heaven. Now if we could just have a little bread to go with it."

Old Curly had a little piece of bread in his pocket. So he broke some off and he pitched it down.

"Glory be to God, the Lord has answered our prayer. He has sent us some bread," said the old robber. Said, "Now if He'll just send us a table to eat it off of," said, "we'll be all right."

Curly he just turned his door go, and down through them limbs it went. Made sech a racket it skeered the robbers off. Well, old Curly jumped down and gathered up their loot. They divided it up, and all of 'em was rich, and they didn't have to steal no more for a living.

Along with the hardships, day-to-day struggles, and wants, the Couches of the mountains had a capacity to learn and a memory to retain the stories and legends of their race. And I can give no better hint of the joy and pleasure these tales brought to the fireside than to repeat here the words of Jim after he had finished a folktale. I asked him how many times he had heard that tale and how the boys and girls liked it. He said, "I have heared and told that story for fifty years. My mother went over that thing time and time again. We'd set just as still as mice and listen at her wind that thing up. And when she'd get through telling three, four like that she'd only have to say 'bed,' and we would get. Best things to pacify chillern I ever saw."

A sampling of the balladry from the family will need to be

spread over a wider variety of material, since there are one hundred different folksongs. The music of the family was gathered in by Tom, the lively father of the household. He sang old ballads in his younger days and shifted with the times to the popular and humorous variety for entertainment and for dancing.

With some effort Jim recalled most of the first one as it was sung in the home up until he was a small boy; then it had sunk out of sight. It is No. 3 in the Child collection, and with a bit of research I find this to be its first appearance in Kentucky. Jim sang to the banjo this ancient ballad of the brave boy who outwits the Devil and escapes his clutches. It is called by Jim

THE DEVIL AND THE SCHOOL CHILD

1. "O where're you goin' there?" said the proud porter gay,
   All alone by the wayside lone;
   "I started to my school," said the child gentlemen,
   And the game feller's walking alone.

2. "What do you have in your bucket?" said the proud porter
   All alone by the wayside lone;   gay,
   "It's vittles for my dinner," said the child gentlemen,
   And the game feller's walking alone.

3. "O won't you give me some?" said the proud porter gay,
   All alone by the wayside lone;
   "No, not a bit o' crumbs," said the child gentlemen,
   And the game feller's walking alone.

4. "I wished I had you in the woods," said the proud porter gay,
   All alone by the wayside lone;
   "With a good gun under my arm," said the child gentlemen,
   And the game feller's walking alone.

5. "With your head broke in two," said the proud porter gay,
   All alone by the wayside lone;

"O a fence rail jobbed down your neck," said the child
And the game feller's walking alone.   gentlemen,

6. "Wished I had you in the sea," said the proud porter gay,
   All alone by the wayside lone;
   "Good board under me," said the child gentlemen,
   And the game feller's walking alone.

7. "Your head turned bottom up," said the proud porter gay,
   All alone by the wayside lone;
   "Yes, and you under the bottom," said the child gentlemen,
   And the game feller's walking alone.

8. "I wished I had you in the well," said the proud porter gay,
   All alone by the wayside lone;
   "But the Devil's chained in Hell," said the child gentlemen,
   And the game feller's walking alone.

The next example is of later date and may be classed as an
imported ballad from Britain. It is not so rare as some of the
Child ballads, this one having been found in three or four
places, including Appalachia, by Cecil Sharp. It was first recorded by Dave to the banjo, but when I showed it to Jim, he
missed a stanza which he could not supply. We set out to old
Tom's cabin and heard him sing it in full.

THE BACHELOR BOY

1. When I was a bachelor boy,
   Courted a maid with a flatterin' tongue;
   Eliza told her I's a hundred and ten;
   I told her I'd marry but I wouldn't tell her when.

2. On Monday morning I married me a wife,
   Fiddlin' and a-dancin' I never saw the like,

THE DEVIL AND THE SCHOOL CHILD

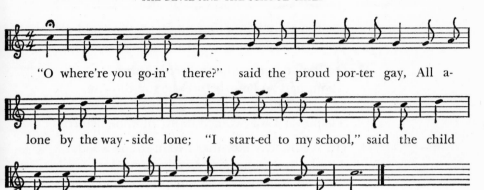

"O where're you go-in' there?" said the proud por-ter gay, All a-

lone by the way-side lone; "I start-ed to my school," said the child

gentle-men, And the game fel-ler's walk-ing a - lone.

THE BACHELOR BOY

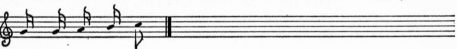

When I was a bache-lor boy, Court-ed a maid with a flat-ter-in' tongue;

E - li-za told her I's a hun-dred and ten; I— told her I'd mar-ry but I

would-n't tell her when.

MINES OF COAL CREEK

I— worked in the mines last Tues-day, I— worked the day be-fore,

At three o'clock on Wednes-day, I'll work in the mines no more.

She tuned up her fiddle and merry she could play,
And I thought to my soul it'd never come day.

3. On Tuesday morning to my sus-prise,
    About half an hour before the sun did rise,
    She tuned up her fife and scolded me more
    Than ever I was scolded in my lifetime before.

4. On Wednesday morning I went to the woods,
    Thinks to myself she'll do me no good,
    I cut me some hickories and a hornbean green,
    I thought it was the toughest I ever had seen.

5. On Thursday morning I carried them home,
    Thinking to myself she's a wife of my own,
    And thought to myself as I laid them by,
    I's expectin' next morning to have them to try.

6. On Friday morning I banged her well,
    Her tongue did rattle like a clapper in a bell,
    I told her the terms, and the terms mought be
    The Devil might have her next morning for me.

7. On Saturday morning the Devil came,
    Took her off in a shower of rain,
    Pass around your brandy bottle, my best friends,
    My hardships have come to an end.

Tragedies figure in the songs of working men, especially mining disasters among Kentucky mountain people. Dave sang this one to the banjo, and when I asked him about it, he said, "They was a boy got killed in the mines, and before he died, he wrote these verses on a rock and left 'em in the mines." This may be a version of the song commemorating the terrible disaster at the Cross Mountain mine in Coal Creek, Tennessee, where 150 men died. The stanza given by Laws in his *Native American Balladry* contains the date 1911.

MINES OF COAL CREEK

1. I worked in the mines last Tuesday,
   I worked the day before,
   At three o'clock on Wednesday,
   I'll work in the mines no more.

2. Shet up in the mines of Coal Creek,
   You know you have to die,
   Just put your trust in Jesus,
   To Heaven your soul shall fly.

3. I got on a train last Wednesday,
   And 'way to the mines did go,
   I come out at four o'clock,
   I never did hear her blow.

4. What hills, what hills, my old truelove,
   That looks so bright and gay?
   That is the hills of sweet heaven,
   Where all the good people live.

5. What hills, what hills, my old truelove,
   That looks so dark and blue?
   That is the hills of a burning Hell,
   Where all mean people go.

6. I hain't grieving over my silver nor gold,
   Neither studying about my home,
   All in the world that's on my mind,
   My darling I left alone.

The popularity of a song like Young Lady in the Bloom of Youth is hard to evaluate except to say that simple people are very sincere and pious in the presence of death. I heard the old man Tom sing parts of this song and say that it was the

best song he knew. Dave sang it without accompaniment and
with the utmost tenderness and feeling. The folk seem to get
a warning from these songs, as well as something more, a kind
of spiritual catharsis from their strains of pity and foreboding.

YOUNG LADY IN THE BLOOM OF YOUTH

1. There was a young lady in the bloom of youth;
   Her age were about sixteen;
   She's called by death and far to go
   From all her friends she seen.

2. Her playmates gathered from far and near,
   They seemed to bow their heads;
   I heard her mother's pitiful groans
   That her poor child was dead.

3. Her oldest brother were standing by,
   His hand upon his breast:
   O pity, Lord, O Lord, forgive
   And take her home to rest.

4. The people gathered from far and near
   To carry away the dead;
   They carried her body to a tomb,
   Where many a tear were shed.

5. O ain't this enough to break friends' hearts,
   To break friends' hearts below?
   To think that we all must die
   And into judgment go.

Murder ballads are continually made up and sung by folk.
This one about Floyd Frazier reached a national distribution
before the folklorists knew when or where the tragedy occurred.
The Couches sang it, and what is more to the point, they knew
the man and the circumstances of the murder. I verified their

statements by going to the Letcher County records and finding
that the man was arrested in 1908 for murdering a mother of
several children and that he was hanged in the county in 1910.
The county court clerk took me to a file room and pulled out
a drawer, and there lay a noose with a tag on it, saying, "Used
in the hanging of Floyd Frazier, 1910." This is Dave's version,
with banjo.

FLOYD FRAZIER

1. Come all you blessed people
   From every nation fair,
   And hear the circumstances
   Of what Floyd Frazier done.

2. He killed poor Ellen Flannery,
   And he knew that he had done wrong;
   He prayed for it to rain
   And wash away the blood.

3. O she had seven little chillern
   From door to door they run;
   They's a-crying for their mother,
   Yet no mother never come.

4. Their little hearts were hungry,
   And they all did fall asleep;
   The morning waked them breaking,
   But no mother never come.

5. He crept into his cabin,
   There for to stay all night;
   He thought his crime was hidden
   From everybody's sight.

6. Fare-you-well, Floyd Frazier,
   Ask God what you have done;
   You killed an innocent woman,
   But you've got the race to run.

7. Floyd Frazier used to be a young man,
   And the girls all knowed him well;
   They hugged and they kissed his cheeks,
   They bid him now farewell.

8. They took him down to the jailhouse,
   They locked him in a cell;
   He killed an innocent woman
   And sent his poor soul to hell.

Even a sampling of songs from the Couches would be incomplete without a lively jig, the kind ideal for whipping a banjo. Old man Tom played the banjo for everything, including the frolics and square dances of the region. Dave took over his job and carried on the duties of musician. With a jig like Sugar Hill and its endless stanzas, and with resting the voice between every stanza, he could probably play a whole square dance set through with one song such as this. Jim, however, recorded this one to banjo accompaniment.

SUGAR HILL

1. Shoo fly lady my girl,
   Shoo fly lady o,
   Shoo fly lady my girl,
   I'm goin' to the sugar store.

2. 'Ts if you want your freedom,
   If you want your fill,
   If you want your eye knocked out,
   Just look on the Sugar Hill.

3. Saw the jaybirds in the mountain,
   Flopping up and down,
   Purty girl in the sugar tree,
   Shaking the sugar down.

YOUNG LADY IN THE BLOOM OF YOUTH

There was a young la-dy in the bloom of youth; Her age were a - bout

six-teen; She's called by death and far to go From all her friends

she seen, From all her friends she seen—, From all her friends

she seen,

FLOYD FRAZIER

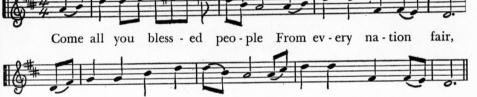

Come all you bless - ed peo - ple From ev - ery na - tion fair,

And hear the cir - cum - stan - ces Of what Floyd Fraz - ier done.

SUGAR HILL

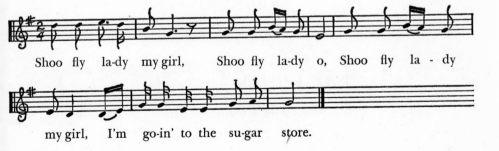

Shoo fly la-dy my girl, Shoo fly la-dy o, Shoo fly la - dy

my girl, I'm go-in' to the su-gar store.

4. 'Ts I set my mill to the grinding,
    Water poured over the dam,
    Thought I'd made a fortune,
    And I married poor Juley Ann.

5. I thought I'd made a fortune
    And never could be sunk;
    I lost it all a-gambling,
    The night that I got drunk.

6. O a jaybird in the mountain,
    Jaybird's trying to crow,
    Dead man's trying to shave himself,
    Blind man's a-trying to sew.

7. O the little bee makes the honey,
    And the big bee makes the comb;
    Poor man fights the battle,
    And the big man stays at home.

8. Jaybird pulls a two-horse load,
    Sparrow, why don't you?
    My neck's so long and slender,
    I'm afraid it'll pull in two.

9. When you go a-courting,
    I'll tell you what to do,
    When you go down to the tailor shop,
    Put on your long-tail blue.

10. When you go a-courting,
    I'll tell you what to say,
    When you go down to the tailor shop,
    Put on your Rebel gray.

11. If I had the money,
    Half that I have lost,
    Buy my wife a shoo-fly dress,
    And I wouldn't care what the cost.

APPENDIX

A list of *The Tales and Songs of the Couch Family* (Kentucky Microcards, series A, no. 30, University of Kentucky Press, 1959), in the order of their appearance, with identifying notes.

23. Arshmen Squirrel Hunting. Type 1227; Motif J-2661.3.
24. Arshmen and the Red Pepper. Motif K-1043.
25. Arshmen and the Gun. Type 1228.
26. Arshman Splitting Rails. Irishman anecdote; no type close.
27. Arshman Never Tard nor Hungry. Type 1561; Motif
    W-111.2.6.
28. I up the Chimley. Witches use magic ointment. No type close.
29. Bridling the Witch. Witch uses man for horse; no type close.
30. To the End of the World. Type 480. Another distinct form
    of No. 2, above.
31. Cat and Rat. Type 2034 (from Archer Taylor, *JAFL*, XLVI
    (1933), 77ff).
32. The Fox and the Cat. Type 20.
33. Tailipoe. Type 366. "Scare" story; see No. 11, above.
34. Fat Man, Fat Man. Type 2028.
35. Chew Tobaccer, Spit, Spit, Spit. Cf. Types 73 and 366.
36. Couch Family Riddles. Forty-five riddles and puzzles, some
    found in Archer Taylor's *English Riddles from Oral Tradition*.
37. Magic Sausage Mill. Type 565.
38. The Three Piggies. Type 124; Motif K-714.2.
39. The Tar-Baby. Type 175; Motif K-741.
40. Granddaddy Bluebeard. Types 955 and 1115.
41. My Mommy Killed Me. Type 720.
42. Rat or Mouse? Contrary couple anecdote. No type close.
43. Sammy and Golder. "What darkened the hole" anecdote.
44. Groundsow Huntin'. Cf. Type 1930. Nonsense narrative.
45. The Colored Preacher. Vilified Devil appears to him. No type
    close, but it is akin to jokes on the parson.
46. Big Frait and Little Frait. Pretending ghost frightened. No
    type close, but it is akin to 1791, next story.
47. Counting the Nuts. Type 1791.
48. Arshman and the Cushaw. Cf. Type 1319.
49. The Holy Ghost. Motif X-434.
50. Seven Days Journey. Mistakes of the guest. No type close.
51. Seven Dead Indians. Type 956B; Motif K-912.
52. Old Indian Binge. Local legend of notorious Indian.
53. We Killed a Bear. Anecdote of cowardly husband.
54. The Hairy Woman. Legend of man mating with wild woman.
55. All at One Shot. Types 1890, 1894, and 1895.
56. Leaping Painter. Local legend of hungry panther.
57. The Magic White Deer. Types 303 and 401.
58. In the Cat Hide. Types 425A and 955. See No. 9, above.

59. The Haunted House. Type 326. See No. 3, above.
60. The Orphant Boys. Motif K-2150.
61. Johnny Sore-Nabel. Second version of Polyphemus, etc. See No. 7, above.

II. SONGS

1. The Devil and the School Child. Child, No. 3. To my knowledge, this is the only text recovered in Kentucky.
2. Lord Batesman. Child, No. 53.
3. Joseph and Mary. Child, No. 54.
4. Little Matty Gross. Child, No. 81.
5. Barbary Allen. Child, No. 84.
6. Hangman. Child, No. 95.
7. Drunkard Blues. Two versions. Child, No. 274.
8. The Devil and the Farmer's Wife. Child, No. 278.
9. The Swapping Boy. English import, with Jack Straw refrain.
10. Old Big Ram. English imported exaggeration.
11. Purty Polly. English import. Last stanzas relate accidental death of murderer.
12. The Bachelor Boy. Marries shrewish woman, runs her off.
13. Rich and Rambling Boy. English import. He gambles and robs on the highway; escapes trial by his high rank; settles down.
14. Sweetheart in the Army. Related to Child, No. 105. Returning soldier tests girl, finds her faithful.
15. The Knoxville Girl. Murder ballad, adapted from the "Oxford Tragedy."
16. Rovin' Gambler.
17. The Wagoner Boy. Jilted by purty Nancy.
18. Wild Bill Jones. Murder ballad.
19. Willow Garden. Murder ballad about Rose Anna Lee.
20. Frankie and Albert. Version of "Frankie and Johnny."
21. Those Brown Eyes. Unrequited love ballad.
22. Jack Was a Lonely Cowboy. Separated by quarrel, he returns to find her dead.
23. The Orphant Girl. She dies by the rich man's door.
24. Brother Green. Civil War battlefield farewell.
25. James A. Garfield. Charles Guiteau mounts the scaffold.
26. Ellen Smith. In disguise, she goes to battle and dies.
27. Mines of Coal Creek. Version of Coal Creek mine disaster.
28. Wreck of Old Ninety-Seven. Ballad of railroad tragedy.

29. When I Left the Blue Ridge Mountains. Parents will not allow Virginia boy to marry their North Carolina daughter.
30. John Hardy. Negro criminal will not lie to his gun.
31. Floyd Frazier. Letcher County hanging ballad.
32. Hiram Hubbard. Rebels hang an innocent man.
33. Kaiser and the Hindenberger. They are panicked when they see the boys of Uncle Sam. Composed by Jim in World War I.
34. Young Lady in the Bloom of Youth. Death of promising girl evokes moral reflections.
35. O Those Tombs. Dead mother mourned for.
36. I Saw a Sight All in a Dream. Dream of dead wife brings repentant thoughts.
37. The Twelve Apostles. Cumulative song; from one to twelve symbols.
38. Bright and Shining City. Depiction of Heaven.
39. Glory Land. Religious hymn.
40. Father Took a Light. Religious hymn.
41. Climbing up Zion's Hills. Religious hymn.
42. The Lifeboat Is Coming. Religious hymn.
43. Lord, I've Started for the Kingdom. Religious hymn.
44. I'm Alone in This World. Religious hymn.
45. O Sinner Man. He will run to the rocks on the Judgment Day.
46. I Got a Hope in That Rock. Religious hymn.
47. Will The Circle Be Unbroken? Questions at death of mother.
48. Praise the Lord I Saw the Light. Religious hymn.
49. Kingdom a-Comin'. Slaves rejoice when the master runs from Lincoln's guns.
50. Yankee Song. Rebels drop their work for guns when the Yankees come.
51. Cumberland Gap. Civil War song.
52. Big Stone Gap. Adaptation of preceding song.
53. Back in the Hills. Boy mourns for dead intended bride.
54. My Daddy Was a Gambler. Son laments his father's teaching.
55. Icy Mountain. Farewell lament.
56. Moonshiner. Successful, but lamenting his calling.
57. Short Life of Trouble. Boy with a broken heart.
58. Chilly Wind. Farewell lament.
59. Darlin' Cory. She goes step by step into crime.
60. Greenback Dollar. Unrequited love lament.
61. In the Pines. Jilted love, with stanzas mourning girl killed by train.
62. Little Birdie. Comparing single with married life.

63. My Trunk is Packed. Farewell lament, composed by Jim Couch.
64. Old Reuben. Railroad man with weakness for drink and women.
65. Good-bye, My Lover. Farewell lament, with stanzas of "Liza Jane."
66. Bald Eagle. Having killed a Negro in a love triangle a long time ago, the singer wishes he were in places far away—possibly a prison song.
67. Paper of Pins. Gifts of increasing value offered for love of the girl; when she accepts keys to his chest, he refuses her.
68. Soldier, Won't You Marry Me? She runs to the store for articles of clothing, only to hear that he is already married.
69. Down the Road. A jig about unusual things happening down the road.
70. Cindy. Humorous banjo jig with "run along home" refrain.
71. Black-Eyed Susie. Humorous banjo piece describing the girl.
72. Blue-Eyed Girl. Humorous banjo jig of jilted love.
73. Georgia Buck. He says, "Never let a woman have her way."
74. Idy Red. Humorous piece describing the girl and her actions.
75. I'm a-Longing for to Go This Road. Ironic love jig describing pretty girl with ugly features.
76. Sourwood Mountain. Banjo square dance jig.
77. Yonder Comes My Love. Same ironic jesting as No. 75, above.
78. Little Brown Jug. Humorous banjo piece.
79. Sugar Hill. Humorous jesting.
80. Shoo Fly. Humorous nonsense jig.
81. Cripple Creek.
82. Old Corn Whisky. It put him in the Harlan jail.
83. Old Coon Dog. He could do various things, but was stolen.
84. Mule Skinner Blues. Logging song.
85. Chisholm Trail. Cowpunching up the trail.
86. Groundhog.
87. Arkansas Traveler. Dialog with singing refrain.
88. Old Dan Tucker.
89. Cold Frosty Morning. Negroes do not have the chores done.
90. Did You Ever See the Devil, Uncle Joe? Humorous Negro piece.
91. Do Johnny Booger. Slave troubles; version of "Run, Nigger, Run."
92. Cock Robin. Children's rhyme about the death of the bird.
93. Tree in the Mountains. Children's cumulative piece.

94. The Old Gray Mare. Troubles with the mare and her hide.
95. The Fox and the Goose. Fox brought one back for the family.
96. The Fox Chase. Narrative with banjo background.
97. Froggy Went a-Courtin'.
98. Funniest Is the Frog. Children's humorous piece.
99. The Little Piggee. Pet pig on the farm.
100. The Cat Played Fiddie on My Fee. Children's cumulative catalog of farm pets.

INDEX

Moonshining: anecdotes by Jim, 60-61; Jim Couch's process of, 61-70; Dave Couch's process of, 70-75
Mountain family: cultural unity of, 51-53; place of parents and children in, 51-52
Mountain folkways, sketch of, 75-79

"Nip, Kink, and Curly" (folktale), 143-46

"Old Indian Binge" (legend), 141-42
"One-Eyed Giant, The" (folktale), 130-34

"Picking Mulberries" (anecdote), 138
Pine Mountain Settlement School: author's home and work at, 1, 19, 37, 50; community activity at, 5; Dave Couch's work at, 38
Play-party, Dave Couch's description of, 31-33
"Polly, Nancy, and Muncimeg" (folktale), 119-23

Rebel Rock, legend of, 87-88
Remedies, various uses of, 95-96
Revenuer. *See* Marshal
Riddles, selection of, 138-40
Riddling, when and where performed, 101-102

Salt, procuring of, 25
School, Dave Couch's attendance at, 28, 30
"Seven Dead Indians" (legend), 140-41
Stewart, Sally Couch: family of, 7; session with, 50
Storytelling, when and why performed, 34, 100-101
"Sugar Hill" (folksong), 154-56

"Tailipoe" (folktale), 127-28
Tales and Songs of the Couch Family, cited, 5, 157
"Two Gals, The" (folktale), 104-108

Wagon making, details of, 25
Weather signs, for planting, hog killing, 34-35
Witchcraft, practices of, 88-95

"Young Lady in the Bloom of Youth" (folksong), 152